Extraordinary Ministry in Ordinary Places

A Guide to Christian Community Development

"I have known Dr. Lula Ballton for over 20 years and she is an outstanding individual. Dr. Ballton is a global leader and role model for our society today. Her passion to advocate utilitarianism has positively changed many lives over the years and she was recently honored for providing 25 years of homes and hope to South Los Angeles. She demonstrates the character and qualities that are so needed today, and organizations throughout the world have recognized her achievements. I am honored to know Dr. Ballton and have been inspired by her ability to remain humble as she continues to make positive change. She is a wife, mother, grandmother, mentor, friend, community builder, and effective leader."

DR. BELINDA ALLEN, *Executive Director*
West Angeles Community Development Corporation

"No one understands better how to transform neglected urban communities than Dr. Lula Ballton. As the Founder and President of the West Angeles Community Development Corporation, she created a premiere entity that has transformed neighborhoods in various cities, including Crenshaw, Los Angeles, San Diego, Memphis, and now Atlanta.

For over 25 years Dr. Ballton has been a catalyst for faith-based community and economic development. In her book, *Extraordinary Ministry in Ordinary Places: A Guide to Christian Community Development,* she shares and draws from her many years and experiences of her work in developing affordable housing units across the country. This book is a refreshing read, written especially for those already involved in or desiring to become involved in community and economic development. It is a must-read for those in the faith community who desire to do "greater works," transformational work in their communities.

Dr. Ballton shares an incredible amount of wisdom as well as practical advice on the subject of Christian Community Development. She also shares some of the pitfalls of urban ministry as a whole and reveals some of the often selfish motives of those who choose to do this work.

I consider her a mentor, and as such, she is using her gift of information to pave easier roads for those who wish to follow in her footsteps.

Ministry in human hands is always a daunting task, but with godly leading, vision, direction, and a touch of His grace we can all do extraordinary ministry even as ordinary people."

ELIZABETH WILSON, *Vice President, Economic Development COGIC Urban Initiatives*

"I remember the day I visited West Angeles Community Development Department to meet with Dr. Lula Ballton. I wore two hats—working for California Assemblymember Marguerite Archie-Hudson and serving as a volunteer with the Jenesse Center. Jenesse was the first domestic violence shelter program founded in South Los Angeles, offering comprehensive programs for families impacted and generally suffering in silence. When I visited Lula she showed me a super thick white notebook; it contained her vision of the church community connecting with the community it served—beyond the Sunday Service. She believed that the church could work to meet the needs of its neighbors with coordinated, excellent services and programs.

At the time her vision was absolutely revolutionary!

I connected with her vision because, in addition to the two hats I mentioned, my family includes generational members of The Churches of God in Christ.

I actually became CEO of Jenesse Center and knew I needed to work with Lula on the issue of domestic violence. We needed to bring domestic violence out of the shadows and put the issue front and center. We realized the church was in a truly unique position to become a powerful partner with us in the fight to eradicate domestic violence. The church is the most enduring institution in our community and because she already had the vision of working more broadly with people beyond church walls, West Angeles CDC and Jenesse were the perfect partners.

Jenesse partnered with West Angeles CDC and wrote a proposal to the State of California and was one of 17 organizations funded to develop a project in unserved communities. We focused on education and training and created a workbook, *Domestic Violence and Unserved/Underserved Populations: Its Roots and Spiritual Cure*. We designed it to be a comprehensive workbook examining domestic violence from spiritual, biblical, theological, and social perspectives.

The workbook is specially designed for clergy, Christian leaders, and church workers. There are sample sermon outlines and sample Sunday School lessons for classes for adults and teenagers. Today this workbook remains a source of centering and connecting the faith-based community and there's no way it could have happened without Dr. Ballton."

KAREN EARLES, *President*
The Jenesse Center

"How do I describe Dr. Lula Ballton? Leader, Activist, Community Organizer, Storyteller, Icon, Disciple of Jesus. All are true, but for me, she is my friend and soulmate, my Sister.

I met this remarkable lady in 2000 at the board meeting of the Christian Community Development Association. I listened to her participation during the meeting and then we sat together afterward for lunch. Within minutes, we both knew we shared a connection birthed deep in our souls. It was born out of a shared passion for justice and combating racism. As women, we were called by God to ministry among the marginalized of society in a Christian universe dominated by male leaders who believed women should not share that rare space. We sat for hours and talked, laughed and told stories, thus beginning a lifelong kinship.

Lula cofounded and served as President of the West Angeles CDC for many years. Her passionate and tireless work to promote the "beloved community" is evidenced in their many projects and initiatives. As Lula said many times, "we are the voice, hands, and feet for those who cannot do for themselves" and she led the CDC effectively to do just that.

Soon after my husband and I moved to the LA area in late 2002, Lula took us on a tour of "her neighborhood." We saw evidence of a swath of the city scarred by a racist system which had redlined the community and moved life-giving jobs to the suburbs. Yet Lula beamed with enthusiasm as we made different stops. What did we see? New low-income housing, a center where job training and entrepreneurship transformed lives, a food and clothing bank for the most vulnerable, retail and office space for community investment, her church actively involved in local ministry, and most importantly, people who had hope.

In short, Dr. Lula Ballton is a national treasure, a gift from Almighty God to all of us who are blessed to know her."

DR. KATHY DUDLEY, *President*
Imani Bridges

"In His demonstrative lesson to His followers, Jesus prayed that God's will would be done on earth as it is in heaven. In this, He asked God the Father to allow His followers to experience a small part of God's heavenly purpose and plan while on this earth. In Southern California, thousands of families in the forgotten neighborhoods of Los Angeles have experienced a little bit of heaven's safety, comfort, and joy as a result of Lula Bailey Ballton's life's work. Wisdom tells us to learn from those who have already walked through the difficult places—this book allows us to do just that as we glean from Lula's decades of experience, expertise, insight, and inspiration. May this book give us guidance, may it challenge us, and may it inspire us to all do extraordinary things in the ordinary places. Amen."

LISA TREVINO CUMMINS, *President*
Urban Strategies

"I have known Dr. Lula Ballton for over 30 years. She is the quintessential expert community development executive director. She has a heart, mind, and soul for serving God's people. God amply prepared Dr. Ballton theologically, sociologically, economically, and spiritually to create, lead, and sustain the West Angeles CDC. Her collaborative, creative, and impactful approaches to community development have had a measurable qualitative and quantitative social impact. The innovative business and social programs have helped stem violence in South Los Angeles, created living-wage jobs, developed housing for low- to moderate-income residents, saved homeowners from losing their homes, and trained thousands at financial literacy workshops.

Dr. Ballton and I served on the Harvard Summer Leadership Board and teaching staff. We set program policy and curriculum, taught classes, and recruited pastors, community development leaders, and board members to learn new methods of community development and civic engagement. The Harvard Summer Leadership Institute trained over 900 Christian leaders in community development. Dr. Ballton is a proven, authentic, out of the box leader/teacher/scholar for the present and future executives of community development."

REV. MARK E. WHITLOCK, MSSE,
Executive Director, Chip Murray Center, School of Religion and Civic Culture, University of Southern California Senior Minister, Reid Temple AME Church

---

"Lula Bailey Ballton has honored God's call with intelligent perseverance as God qualified her to do this work over the past 25 years. With faith walking and "truth to power talking," she has embodied and created the true Christian Community and Economic Development model.

Lula has used her giftings as a creative genius and effective communicator to help establish the kingdom of God here on earth. In this book, she has made the arduous process of establishing and sustaining Christian Community and Economic Development look easy. Her gift to future visionaries is to "write the vision, make it plain so you can run with it, because faith works when you work it."

ANNE COGGS MYLES SMITH, M.A.T., M.S.,
Juris Doctorate

"*Extraordinary Ministry in Ordinary Places* captures the essence of Lula Ballton's outstanding work in South Los Angeles. She developed a stunning housing development for low-income senior citizens with all the amenities of a private market condominium. Her love and respect for this community and its inhabitants shine through in the residents' private and communal spaces.

I met Lula when her project was a hope and a dream. Lula was a student in the Summer Leadership Institute (SLI) which I led at Harvard University Divinity School. Over several years she developed and implemented her plan.

Lula Ballton is a shining example of the role that SLI played in helping ministers implement economic development projects. She became a lecturer in the Summer Leadership Institute. Lula was respected and admired by Institute participants for her dynamic and candid presentations. She has made a lasting contribution to economic development in African-American churches."

PRESTON N. WILLIAMS, *Houghton Professor Emeritus*
Harvard Divinity School, Harvard University

Extraordinary Ministry in Ordinary Places

A Guide to Christian Community Development

LULA BAILEY BALLTON
with Rae Lynne Johnson

Urban Ministries, Inc.

Published in the United States by Urban Ministries, Inc.
P. O. Box 436987
Chicago, IL 60643
www.urbanministries.com 1-800-860-8642

ISBN 978-1-68353-526-3 (paperback)
ISBN 978-1-68353-527-0 (ebook)

Library of Congress Cataloguing-in-Publication Data
Ballton, Lula Bailey 1947 -
Extraordinary Ministry in Ordinary Places: A Guide to Christian
Community Development/Lula Bailey Ballton
p. cm.
Community Development. 2. Christian Ministry.
3. Economic Justice. 4. Social Justice.   I. Title.

Library of Congress Control Number: 2019950207
Unless otherwise noted, Scripture quotations and passages are
from the King James Version (KJV), the Contemporary English
Version (CEV), and the New King James Version® of the Bible.
Copyright © 1982 by Thomas Nelson, Inc. Used by permission.
All rights reserved.

Grateful acknowledgment is made to Carter McNamara,
author of Field Guide to Nonprofit Program Design,
Marketing and Evaluation.

10 9 8 7 6 5 4 3 2 1
First Edition

Cover design by Laura Duffy
Book design by Astrid Lewis Reedy
Editing by Mary C. Lewis, MCL Editing, Etc.

Printed in the United States of America

DEDICATION

I dedicate this book to my family who gave me the love,
support, and space to dream big and walk toward God's
light. THANK YOU!

To Carl Ballton, my life partner and husband of 50 years,
who gave *me both financial and emotional support to do
this work for 25 years—one-half of our married life!* I love,
respect, and hope I honor you with my work and this
book.

To my children, Jabari, Issa Carl, and Micah, who
supported me and my vision for community development.
Even when they wanted me for theirs alone, they shared
me with a variety of community people and issues. I
wanted our community to be better for you! You were my
motivation and the wind beneath my wings. THANK YOU!

To my fore-parents, who taught me that it was
my responsibility, not to complain about the world's
condition, but to change it. THANK YOU!

I further dedicate this book to the friends, colleagues,
community, and corporate partners who made our work
successful. THANK YOU!

TABLE OF CONTENTS

FOREWORD

Extraordinary Ministry in Ordinary Places is a not-so-ordinary book written by Lula Bailey Ballton, the first Executive Director of the West Angeles Christian Community Development Corporation. This book was birthed out of the desire to see change fostered by community and economic development for the residents of South Los Angeles.

The West Angeles Christian Community Development Corporation was led by Lula Ballton from its inception to manage, administer, and distribute our church benevolence to both our congregation and an outreach ministry to the community. The goals were to establish and promote economic development, civic and social justice as well as a caring outreach to the poor and disenfranchised in our community. Dr. Ballton would summarize her vision by saying, "We serve God and love people."

The CDC Mission Statement reads:

"The call of the mission of West Angeles Community Development Corporation is to increase social and economic justice, demonstrate compassion, and alleviate poverty as tangible expressions of the Kingdom of God through the vehicle of community development."

This mission remains the driver of the CDC's work.

The CDC has established and created numerous real estate and community-based programs. The first of the real estate programs which started to develop legs was the makeover of two empty lots, chronic eyesores, trash-filled and desolate home of transients, weeds, and trouble, across the street from Manual Arts High School and replaced with the first development of low-income West Angeles Homes. The second project of the CDC was West Angeles Parklane Apartments, located in what we call, "The Jungle," once considered unsafe. The Jungle now has multi-ethnicities residing and thriving. The next real estate project was the West Angeles Villas, a senior housing complex. The WACDC's multifaceted community-based programs involve Homeownership Centers, offering services on ownership, entrepreneurial training, dispute resolution, a real estate development team, and much more. Dr. Ballton is now the CEO Emeritus of the WACDC and also holds the position of Director, Community and Economic Development for the Church of God in Christ International. Dr. Ballton's projects for the COGIC include Mason Village Housing in Memphis, TN, allowing our denomination the opportunity to partner with the city of Memphis and John Stanley, thus helping many low-income families to call Mason Village home. The village consists of 77 townhouses on seven acres.

Not only has Dr. Ballton attained this vision by creating cutting-edge programs with the idea of social justice via community transformation, she has managed to do so by attaining and maintaining local control of capital and management of community assets. Dr. Ballton has received numerous awards, honors, and Best Practice Commendations. She serves on numerous boards and professional organizations, including Links organizations, the U.S. Department of Justice, Black Women Lawyers, Advisory Board of the Alpha Kappa Educational Advancement Foundation, Inc., Harvard Divinity School, to name a few. With an MA in Communications, she successfully led a 14-year career as a professor at various state and community colleges, served as Director of Education for Chicago Urban League, and attained her Juris Doctorate from UCLA School of Law.

We can see the successes of Dr. Ballton and her desire to share the road map she has been blessed to follow in uplifting the community through community and economic development. The road map that has been created by God has blessed Lula Bailey Ballton with the divine ability to do as Jesus did, "We serve God and love people." If you have the same desires and dreams to change your community as Dr. Lula Bailey Ballton has done, then this book will be the guide to your road. If you put these practices into place, you will truly have an "Extraordinary Ministry in Ordinary Places."

—BISHOP CHARLES E. BLAKE SR., *Pastor*
West Angeles Church of God in Christ
Presiding Bishop, Church of God In Christ, Inc.,
7th in Succession

HOW TO USE
EXTRAORDINARY MINISTRY
IN ORDINARY PLACES

Extraordinary Ministry in Ordinary Places: A Guide to Christian Community Development offers a unique opportunity. Those interested in starting a Christian Community Development Corporation—church members, community leaders, graduate students, and working professionals in social work, public health, city planning, and other fields—now have a multifaceted book at your disposal. *Extraordinary Ministry* gives you actual experiences to inspire you and best practices to guide you.

A few tips, then, to help you use this book. You'll find four sections in the Table of Contents:

1. Administration
2. Economic Development
3. Program Development
4. How to Start Your Christian CDC: Steps to Follow

Administration, Economic Development, and Program Development correspond to the basic components of most community development corporations—the bones, so to speak, of this kind of nonprofit organization. And in order to help put "meat" on the bones, we've provided department overviews and profiles of staff members of the West Angeles Community Development Corporation (WACDC). Along with others at the WACDC, their dedication and expertise, led by the incomparable Cofounder and Executive Director Dr. Lula Bailey Ballton, resulted in many great achievements for the residents of West Angeles, a South Central Los Angeles community. (We've included some of those achievements in the "Introduction".) The staff profiles found in the Administration, Economic Development, and Program Development sections help you gain a specific understanding of what evolved and remains a landmark example of a Christian Community Development Corporation.

You're probably wondering: How could my church step forward and form a Christian Community Development Corporation? Answering that question requires answers to many other questions about forming a board, agreeing on the Christian CDC's vision, putting together a mission statement, establishing a legal component, obtaining funding, hiring staff, gathering volunteers, and other elements. We know you'll face challenges and that's why this book comes ready with more assistance. The Steps to Follow section will guide you through these and other issues you'll need to untangle as your Christian CDC goes through its early years of operation.

As you establish, form, and launch the administration, economic development, and program development of your Christian Community Development Corporation, we encourage you to keep using this book. We hope the profiles will motivate you as you create your own staff experiences. We trust the Steps to Follow section will provide definite procedures for your CDC to use.

Most of all, since this is about *Christian* CDCs, we urge you to remain prayerful in your pursuit of healthy communities. God will always hear your prayers and illuminate your path! (Psalm 18:28)

—THE EDITORIAL TEAM

ACKNOWLEDGMENTS

I am honored that **Bishop Charles Blake Sr.**, had a vision for the West Angeles Church Community Ministry in Los Angeles and he chose me to lead it. I thank God that my pastor, Bishop Blake, identified me as his choice to establish the community development ministry at West Angeles Church.

Rev. John M. Perkins also identified me to be a leader in Christian Community Development. In doing so, he set to teaching me the biblical basis for Christian Community Development and how to implement such a program. As the Lord led these two men to direct and teach me, He changed my life forever. I am no longer only a professor of communication or a lawyer, but an active member of the ministry of Jesus Christ. What an honor to be led by and work with those anointed for and committed to Kingdom work.

By God's grace this book came about by a miracle in Chicago. (That will be told in a different forthcoming book.) Through an act of God I met the people who made this book happen. UMI founder, **Dr. Melvin Banks**; UMI CEO, Attorney **C. Jeffrey Wright**; and UMI Publishing Director, **Annette V. Leach**, transformed my ministry discussion, countless seminars, community stories/legends to this format...A BOOK! Editors **Mary Lewis and Rae Lynne Johnson** read, listened to, and organized my thoughts, and interviewed former staff members at WACDC as I requested.

I want to acknowledge the many staff and volunteers who put operational legs on and wrapped programs around my ideas and vision of developing our community by our community for 25 years. Special acknowledgment and thank-you's to Dr. Desireé Tillman Jones, our first lay chair-person; Minister Anne Coggs Smith, our first Board Member; Grant Power, an initial thought and prayer partner; and staff member par excellence **Claudia L. Jones** for creating, organizing, implementing, and managing the systems that made our CDC work! Claudia's competence and integrity created a business culture we were all proud to be a part of. I also want to acknowledge **Paul Turner** whom I hired from Eastern Seminary in Pennsylvania to come home to California and assist me at the Union Rescue Mission. He was *my first hire* at West Angeles CDC and our first manager of economic development.

By God's grace we did the work. We created and have sustained the West Angeles CDC for 25 years.

By God's miracle we were able to come together to create this book to tell our story, so other Believers can replicate this Community Development Ministry, responding to His call.

"Children, you show love for others by truly helping them, and not merely talking about it" (1 John 3:18, CEV).

—DR. LULA BAILEY BALLTON

INTRODUCTION

Development Is Ministry—
The Theology of Economic Development

A Case from Vision to Implementation

Extraordinary Ministry in Ordinary Places: A Guide to Christian Community Development explores the scriptural and real-world basis for a clear vision of God's purpose for us as it relates to our dominion over and development of His earth and His people. It is a discussion of social and economic justice as stewardship. The three-part book features profiles of staff members at West Angeles Community Development Corporation (WACDC), which I established for Bishop Charles Blake, pastor of West Angeles Church of God in Christ. Thanks to the efforts of Sam Hughes, Claudia Jones, Paul Turner, and others at WACDC, their leading role in administrative development, economic development, and program development helped bring about an applied theology of Christian community development in South Central Los Angeles. The profiles are followed by "Steps to Follow," so you can establish or reinvigorate a community development corporation in your own community based on your particular circumstances and resources. "How to Use *Extraordinary Ministry in Ordinary Places*" will give you more details.

What is and is not Christian community development? Before we examine that, let's dive into some background and theory so you can increase your awareness of what's involved in this undertaking and whet your appetite for how this book can help you and your church.

> *"Where there is no vision, the people perish."*
> (Proverbs 29:18, KJV)

I began my journey with the Lord to do economic development at a time that many would consider to be late in the game. In fact, I did not begin law school until age 40. When the Lord began prompting me to build healthy communities, I had been married for a number of years, had three children, and had been a college professor for 12 years. I was an attorney with a solid career that did not seem to allow for major life changes. With my corporate lawyer's salary, I was busy buying a car, furniture, paying for Christian private schools for three children, and acquiring other stuff. Yet, the Lord reminded me that life was more than just acquiring "more stuff." The Lord wanted me to care for the poor and to fight injustice. In the book of Amos, people tithed and gave offerings to God, but their gifts stunk because they did not take care of the poor (see Amos 5:21–24). God does not want His people to forget about those who are facing financial difficulties and hard times. He wants the entire community to be whole!

I believe that living in healthy communities helps to make God's vision real for people. By way of example, let us take a look at Ezekiel 22:24–31 (NKJV):

> [24] *"Son of man, say to her: 'You* are *a land that is not cleansed or rained on in the day of indignation.'* [25] *The conspiracy of her prophets in her midst is like a roaring lion tearing the prey; they have devoured people; they have taken treasure and precious things; they have made many widows in her midst.* [26] *Her priests have violated My law and profaned My holy things; they have*

not distinguished between the holy and unholy, nor have they made known the difference *between the unclean and the clean; and they have hidden their eyes from My Sabbaths, so that I am profaned among them.* ²⁷ *Her princes in her midst are like wolves tearing the prey, to shed blood, to destroy people, and to get dishonest gain.* ²⁸ *Her prophets plastered them with untempered mortar, seeing false visions, and divining lies for them, saying, 'Thus says the Lord GOD,' when the LORD had not spoken.* ²⁹ *The people of the land have used oppressions, committed robbery, and mistreated the poor and needy; and they wrongfully oppress the stranger.* ³⁰ *So I sought for a man among them who would make a wall, and stand in the gap before Me on behalf of the land, that I should not destroy it; but I found no one.* ³¹ *Therefore I have poured out My indignation on them; I have consumed them with the fire of My wrath; and I have recompensed their deeds on their own heads," says the Lord GOD.*

In the situation described above, the princes (think: politicians) were dishonest. The priests (preachers and pastors) were whitewashing the negative situation and proclaiming things that God did not say. The people of the land were oppressing the immigrants. The Lord sought someone to stand in the gap to prevent His judgment.

As was the case in the days of the Old Testament prophets, our world is filled with corruption and unrighteousness. The poor and the needy are still being mistreated; immigrants are still being oppressed and God is not pleased. I believe that the people of God can be the gap-fillers, interceding for a return to righteousness so that God will not destroy the land. A special burden should be felt by all leaders, pastors, and other brothers and sisters in the ministry to be the gap-fillers for whom God is looking.

What is the center of your community?

Many African-Americans grew up with the Christian Church as the center of their communities. People were identified by the content of their character rather than by the color of their skin, their family history, or their socioeconomic status. A person could be a house-keeper by day and serve as the president of the Sunday School at church. He or she could clean up the post office at night and still chair the deacon or deaconess board. Participation in these community roles was based on character, faithfulness, and the pursuit of God rather than on pedigree.

In these communities, discerning individuals could identify the future preachers, teachers, lawyers, businesspeople, and other role players by examining the gifts displayed by young people. An identity was created for these young people within the context of their communities and their gifts were affirmed by the broader community. Moreover, communities were organized in a manner where everyone participated. If little Johnny or Suzie misbehaved at school or within the neighborhood, then he or she might face the possibility of being disciplined by any number of responsible adults in the community.

When African-Americans of previous generations got ready for college, the expectation was that they would return to their communities. The concept of "our" was very important. If you were "our doctor," for example, then you were supposed to come back to the community. When students went away to college, their communities would send them care packages on a regular basis. The messages "you belong" and "you will always have a place here" were constantly reinforced. The seeds of the Beloved Community spoken of in Nehemiah 8:10 were planted in previous generations of African-Americans.

At some point in the latter half of the 20th century, the vision was lost. For example, later generations of African-Americans were sent away from their communities as an escape and were taught to be ashamed of who they were and where they came from. A void was created that needed to be filled. People of other ethnicities began to find economic success through meeting the needs of African-Americans right in their own communities. The proliferation within African-American communities of stores, dry cleaners, gas stations, and the like with owners of non-African descent angered many African-Americans within those communities. Yet, the reality was that few young African-American students and other young people were sent away with the vision of returning to start businesses within the communities that they left behind. Children were told to grow up, get an education, and get out of here. They did and when these young people went away, many ran into glass ceilings and ended up in places where they were not welcome and where they would try not to congregate and draw negative attention from the majority culture. Well, we must now put a stop to the forces that fracture and tear down our communities and recover the vision of the Beloved Community.

I have remained in my community and dedicated my life to realizing a positive vision for its future. My great-grandfather was a slave who made a deal with his master to become a free Presbyterian minister. Of the five generations of my family members, none have moved out of their communities. If everyone who has grown up in a certain community refuses to live in and participate in that community, then there is no way for the community to remain vital.

What is your vision?

Individuals, families, and communities all require clear vision in order to remain healthy. What is your personal vision? What is your vision for your family? What is your vision for your children? What do you see for your grandchildren? What is your vision for your community? Where do you want to be five years from now, ten years from now, fifteen years from now, and beyond? Your vision should be more than simply a list of material things, such as houses, cars, property, or finances to acquire in life. Vision is where you want to be in the future. Have you given much thought to your vision? If you have, then great! May God help you to realize your vision. If you have not yet given much thought to your personal vision, then it is not too late to begin to think about the direction in which your life is headed.

A vision is an aspirational objective. It is an optimal desired state yet to be attained. Put simply, a vision defines where a person or group wants to be in the future. The notion of vision is very important, biblically and historically. The Old Testament prophets, for example, often envisioned a future free from pain, poverty, oppression, and injustice. More recently, the "Beloved Community" was a vision based on Scripture and popularized by Dr. Martin Luther King Jr., during the American Civil Rights Movement of the 1950s and 1960s. The vision of peace, nonviolence, racial equality, and economic justice had the Christian notion of *agape* (God's perfect and selfless love) at its core and was for King a realizable goal for African-Americans and all people of goodwill.

A Christian community development corporation needs to explore and identify its vision. This was among the first tasks the staff at the WACDC had to grapple with, and it will be one of your CDC's first tasks as well. Here is the call portion of the WAC-DC mission statement: "The mission of West Angeles Community Development Corporation is to increase social and economic justice, demonstrate compassion, and alleviate poverty as tangible expressions of the Kingdom of God through the vehicle of Community Development." For more information, visit the WACDC's website: *www.westangelescdc.org*.

God wants to use you!

God wants to use you to make a difference. Do not limit yourself. It is never too late to start moving in the right direction! Remember that I was already 40 years old when I went to law school. Why not plant a seed right now into the realization of your vision? The words of Galatians 6:7 are so appropriate: *"Do not be deceived, God is not mocked; for whatever a man sows, that he will also reap."*

So, what do you have to plant? God has given you time. He has given you various gifts and talents. There are physical and intellectual resources at your disposal that can help your community. Where are you in the realization of the vision that God has for you? We need to access all of our talents, abilities, and gifts in order to leverage these assets to create wealth and wholeness in our communities.

What is community development?

The traditional/formal definition of "community development" is a process where community members come together to take collective action and generate solutions to common problems. Community well-being—economic, social, environmental, and cultural— often evolves from this type of collective action being taken at the grassroots level.

The broadest definition is tremendously wide. It includes intentional social and economic well-being, the sustainability of our communities in their current geographic and economic configuration, and everything that impacts our housing stock.

However, the most basic definition is simply, "the activity of working with people from a particular area in order to try to improve their quality of life" (*Cambridge Business English Dictionary*).

THERE IS A DIFFERENCE BETWEEN GENERAL AND CHRISTIAN COMMUNITY DEVELOPMENT!

Let us begin with what Christian community development is NOT; then we can look at what it IS.

Christian Community Development is NOT...

There are many misconceptions about Christian community development. Let us address a few erroneous understandings before defining exactly what Christian community development is in fact. Christian community development is not:

- Economic growth;
- Doing to or for people what they can do for themselves right now;
- Merely bringing jobs and business to a neighborhood;
- Perfect equality (in terms of modernization, industrialization, or urbanization);
- A vehicle designed to generate money to build our church and other buildings; or
- Another way to get money from the programs designed for the poor to enhance middle-class ministries.

Building a community for Christ is broader than simply making money or creating jobs in that community. Good development does take money, but not necessarily a lot of it. **What is needed most is a group of dedicated, like-minded people working together to turn a good idea, or more accurately a "God" idea, into reality.** Christian community development requires sensitivity to God's heart for people. It requires concern for the whole person (spirit, mind, and body), and it places wealth generation within the context of self-determination and economic justice. Furthermore, one should not get involved in community development for the wrong reasons. Sometimes money can be distracting to those who are given stewardship over a CDC, but it is very important that money acquired from governmental and other sources be used for the purposes for which it was given rather than other purposes (no matter how "noble" one's intentions). While taking shortcuts may appear to bring success at a faster rate, shortcuts based on the lowering of ethical standards will lead to a place of destruction. Galatians 6:7 remains true when negative seeds are planted just as it is true for good seeds.

Christian Community Development IS...

- Creating better communities bit by bit for the glory of the Lord;
- A process that allows people to reach for all God intends for them as God's children;
- A process of CHANGE which causes people to lose their limitations;
- A process in which people move from a place where they are objects of other people's agendas to a new place where they *set their own agenda under the Lordship of Jesus Christ*;
- MINISTRY: The infusion of hope, meaning, and purpose. It transforms people's self-perception, attitude, and experience from *despair and inferiority* to *hope and justice*.

Building a community for Christ will empower people and inspire them to become more than they ever thought possible. When people get out of the boxes created by their own limited thinking, they will realize that they can accomplish extraordinary things with God's help. Furthermore, because Christ will be at the center of the community development process, people will grow in their faith. They will also improve in their feelings about themselves. They will have better relationships with others and expand in their capacity to love the community. Building a community for Christ is about more than making money.

21

What does a community development corporation DO?

A CDC engages in a range of activities. Typical CDC activities include:

- Economic development (such as job training, real estate development, creating businesses, or attracting new businesses to the community);
- Community projects (for example, cleanup, beautification initiatives, etc.);
- Social services (such as operating shelters for homeless people, providing assistance with paying for utility bills, etc.); and
- Educational programs (for example, after-school help, substance abuse awareness programs, etc.)

Of course, the above list is just a small sampling of what CDCs do in general. Some have a very broad objective while others may have a narrower focus. I encourage you to look at the structures of some CDCs with which you are already familiar.

In an effort to provide concrete examples, here are some specific activities that the West Angeles CDC (WACDC) pursued during my time there as executive director. Of course, when I helped Bishop Blake establish the WACDC in 1993 we did not develop, fund, and launch all of these activities at once; it took us some time to experience a learning curve of both successes and mistakes. But after several years, the West Angeles CDC was involved in the following activities:

Community Assistance
- Emergency and social services
- Senior Care Program
- SHARE: Food Buyer Cooperative
- Energy Assistance Program
- Housing and job referrals

Economic Development
- Commercial real estate development
- Entrepreneur/small business technical assistance
- Stimulation of leading business sectors

Commercial Real Estate Development
- West Angeles/Union Bank Plaza, located at Crenshaw and Jefferson
- Home Depot Shopping Center, at Slauson and Western
- The Curve Mixed Use Plaza, at Crenshaw and 54th Street

Training and Employment (Services Offered in Four Phases)
- Outreach, intake, and assessment
- Development of life skills
- Development of job skills
- Case management – job placement, job retention

Mediation Center
- PeaceMaker Violence Prevention Training Program
  – for all school-age levels
- Community mediator certificate training
  – 30-hour state program
- Certified mediator advanced training
  – professional enhancement seminars
- Community mediation services
  – mediations, conciliations, and arbitration services

Affordable Housing Developments

- West A Homes: large families or families with handicapped members
- Parklane Apartments: families with children
- West Angeles Villas: seniors

Home Ownership Center

- Homebuyer education and training classes
- Acquire and rehab single-family residences to sell to low- to moderate-income families
- Mortgage prequalifying service to prospective home buyers
- Financial education

Development Consultants

- Fee-based
- Joint venture

We need to stand in the gap so that healthy communities may thrive once again. God is calling us to stand in the gap. We must build expectations of success in future generations. We cannot allow others to give our children limited visions grounded in racism, poverty, etc. I believe that we must strive to see economic and social justice in the communities where we live. Economic and social justice involves fairness in business, fairness in the courts, fairness in our schools, and fairness in the vast world of opportunity in which we live.

I invite you to dig deeply into this book and discover how establishing a Christian community development corporation might help you and your church plant the seeds for a renewed community in your midst. Will you stand in the gap and work toward realizing the vision of the Beloved Community?

—DR. LULA BAILEY BALLTON

ADMINISTRATION DEPARTMENT

West Angeles CDC, in keeping with its vision and mission of building a stronger community, continues its original strategic focus of demonstrating compassion, pursuing social and economic justice, and reducing poverty as an expression of the Kingdom of God through the vehicle of Community Development.

The Administration Department is the engine of the CDC vehicle that allows the organization to execute its strategic plan as a blueprint for key management decisions and actions. A major ongoing challenge to the West Angeles CDC is to expand its operations at a prudent pace without losing major opportunities in community development. In particular, we continue to search for better ways to support our growth with a strong operational base.

To achieve this goal, the WACDC's Administration Department focuses on four main functions:

- POLICIES AND PROCEDURES (Operations and Planning)
- FUNDRAISING (Annual Unity Awards Banquet)

- FISCAL MANAGEMENT (Accounting Procedures and Financial Statements)
- COMMUNITY ADVOCACY (Political and Social Concerns)

In addition to our four main functions, the Administration Department is responsible for providing expanded community and family services, by partnering with other nonprofit organizations.

CLAUDIA JONES
Chief Operating Officer
1994 – 2008

Like many new organizations, West Angeles Community Development Corporation epitomized humble beginnings in 1994. Claudia Jones, Lula Ballton's first administrative assistant, one of the first four staffers at the new CDC recalls, "We had one office and one desk and one phone. The phone would ring and I would answer the phone, and I would tell them, 'Hold on, let me see if she's in her office,' and then I would pass it to her. She sat on one side of the desk. I sat on the other." Also sharing the desk, one using a chair, the other, a love seat were Grant Powers, churning out grant proposals to acquire funding, and Paul Turner, leveraging his economic development expertise to acquire funding.

While their office was modest, their mission—to increase social and economic justice, demonstrate compassion, and alleviate poverty as tangible expressions of the Kingdom of God through the vehicle of community development—was bold. The first requirement in their quest was to determine the actual needs of the community. "We wanted to serve the community, but what do they need? Do they need jobs, or do they need food, or do they need a babysitter while they go to work?" Securing college interns, WACDC did surveys in the community to find out.

Attract Motivated Volunteers

As a picture of the actual—rather than perceived—needs in the community emerged, WACDC developed relevant programs to address the pain points of the people they sought to serve. A serendipitous benefit of on-point programs was their ability to attract a slew of volunteers. One such program was domestic violence advocacy. WACDC partnered with another nonprofit organization and co-wrote a grant proposal which resulted in funding from the state to do domestic violence training. After posting a notice in the West Angeles Church bulletin about the program, WACDC attracted many interested volunteers who eagerly went through domestic violence advocacy training and subsequently worked in the program.

Each successful program increased WACDC's growing reputation in the community which, as time went on, made attracting volunteers easier. The CDC also acquired volunteers by providing opportunities for people who had to do community service. Eventually, WACDC was contacted by other agencies inquiring about the availability of volunteer opportunities.

To their credit, West Angeles CDC board members also served as volunteers. The CDC offered "law day" several times a year, due to its popularity, where members of the community could come to receive free legal advice. "We had a working board," says Claudia. "Our board would help us. We had a few attorneys on the board, so they would assist us in some of those efforts."

Another way of procuring additional human resources with no cost to the CDC was by partnering with other nonprofits to work on projects together, each partner enhancing the efforts of the other. An added benefit of these partnerships was the ability to get more funds for both organizations because jointly they had more to offer.

Claudia cautions, however, that it is not enough to attract volunteers; you must have a good screening process because volunteers are "representing you" in the community. "If you have someone who comes in and has the wrong attitude or does not have the same spirit as what you're trying to portray in the community, well that's a problem." For example, you don't want "Mr. Grinch" handing out bags of food to the homeless on distribution days.

Claudia suggests the following for inclusion in a volunteer screening process:

- Make sure a potential volunteer knows your vision and mission and buys into both
- Make sure they have demonstrated capability for the task(s) you plan to assign
- Make sure their personality is suited to the task
- Even though it is for a volunteer position, select candidates who can maintain your standards of excellence
- If you suspect they are not a good fit, resist the urge to place them in the position

Don't Dwell on Disappointments

According to Claudia, one highly developed program, foster care, attracted an "overwhelming number" of volunteers because it responded to an urgent need in the community.

Unfortunately, WACDC was unable to roll out the program. The County of Los Angeles offered a training program for people who wanted to be foster parents. The County also licensed qualified organizations to administer this foster parent program.

Claudia and the volunteers, many from West Angeles Church, went through the County's training. Claudia also wrote a grant proposal to acquire funds for WACDC to become licensed administrators of the county's foster parent program. She went through extensive additional administrative training, wrote a voluminous proposal, and organized the volunteers. WACDC and the volunteers dedicated a great deal of time, work, and commitment to the foster care program.

Then "at the last minute," Claudia says, "the County stopped licensing any organizations to administer the program." Even though WACDC already had very successful programs, such as housing, economic development, and mediation programs, after so much time and emotional investment, not being able to roll out the foster care was a blow. "That was kind of heartbreaking to me." The lesson? When plans derail, let the vision and mission drive you forward.

Select Your Board Strategically

Indeed, vision and mission must be an ever-present focus for driving the entire organization, starting with the board of directors. Turning to the subject of board members, Claudia had this to say: "I think the one important thing is to have a working board. I mean it's sometimes easy to get people who want to dictate." There are people who want to be on a board purely for the prestige. WACDC was fortunate, however, to have board members who not only supported the CDC, its mission, and its staff but also, Claudia points out, were willing "to actually get their hands dirty" assisting with projects wherever needed. West Angeles CDC hosts an annual awards gala, one of the primary sources of unrestricted funds—funds that can support staff and projects not specifically funded by grants. Claudia notes that board members are responsible for selling more tickets and tables than the staff.

There are other strategic ways board members can assist. "We had some board members that were in the banking field. So we had good relationships with different bankers. We had a housing department, so we had some of our board members and staff who had relationships with different agencies or organizations that would support housing. A lot of it has to do with your relationships in the community." Claudia gives an example: "If you're trying to raise funds to open a dog shelter, you've got to have some kind of relationships with people in that industry."

Retreat to Advance

One way West Angeles CDC fostered relationships internally was through board retreats and staff retreats, for which Claudia was responsible. "We would do everything we could to make sure our staff and our board stayed on board. And we'd have fun. I was responsible for our staff retreats and I tried to have two a year, one for learning and one for fun." The retreats built camaraderie. "When you're working in any nonprofit, you always have more on your plate than the average person. So when you're working at your responsibility, you don't really have that much time to socialize or go to other departments." Retreats occurred at a variety of venues from hotels to popular local attractions to picnics at the park. There were games, prizes, gifts, and good food.

The CDC would often ask organizations they worked with to sponsor staff retreats, so costs were minimal. The retreats were opportunities to not only build relationships and unwind but to find out what was happening in different departments of the CDC in more depth than what could occur at weekly staff meetings. It was also a time to review the vision and mission of the CDC. Attendees reviewed successes from the previous year and evaluated how they lined up with the mission statement.

Board retreats are also a good time to reassess the organization every five years. It takes one-to-two years to get a program started, and another two years or so to make it successful. So five years is a good time for reevaluation. Notwithstanding these important objectives that help to advance a CDC, the key to any good retreat, Claudia insists, is to "make it fun."

Keep Meticulous Records

Claudia offers this final word of advice to advance CDCs: Keep meticulous records. "You've got to keep data in order to know where you are." Data measure the accuracy of your success rate, allowing the organization to look at itself and see what is actually there. Data are also critical to facilitate the solicitation of more funding. Donors want to know what you're going to do with the money they give to the organization. The best indicator they will have of what they can expect from you in the future is what you've done in the past. Data allow you to say, "It was successful, and if we had this much more money, we can make it more successful." Good, accurate data allow the organization to keep growing. WACDC makes sharing data with donors an important part of its annual fundraising gala.

Data are not only invaluable to increase funding, but this information also supports necessary reporting metrics for the board of directors, who are ultimately responsible for the organization. Accurate data allow the board to make critical evaluations of a CDC and devise course corrections as necessary. A CDC is also responsible to the community. Figures must be accurate and precise for auditors: federal auditors, state auditors, foundation auditors. Claudia points out, "They are going to come in; they want to look at your books and to look at what you're doing." Accurate data are both a measure of effectiveness and a barometer for growth.

Add Simple Ingredients for Effectiveness

When asked about the key ingredients for WACDC's effectiveness and durability, after a moment of reflection, Claudia responds, "I think just the sense of the programs, the professionalism of the staff—the leadership meeting the wants of the community." She shares an example of one of West Angeles CDC's most popular programs, brilliant in its simplicity, beautifully targeted to a need in the community. During tax season, WACDC provided tax counselors to serve the community and did simple taxes for free. It was a little thing that made a big impact in the community. "The community remembered, 'I can go to the CDC and get my taxes done.' Little things like that. When you meet the community's needs, you get the word out."

Finding those little, relevant needs helps with the diversity of the organization and the programs, contributing to the success of both. As examples of enduring organizations, consider the Red Cross and Goodwill, both huge nonprofit organizations, but they had to start somewhere, and they started small. When it became obvious to the communities they served that they were doing good, effective work, then people started supporting them. Now they are international organizations. It's the same process for smaller organizations—find what works. "If [a program] doesn't work," Claudia advises, "get rid of it, and start something else."

And when it does work, keep doing it. Claudia is retired and living in Atlanta, but she still works at a CDC, focused on domestic violence advocacy, just like the program she started at West Angeles CDC. She says she's been working ten years after retirement because "once it's in you, you just keep doing it."

ROBERT J. NORRIS JR.
Director of Operations
2008 – 2011

For Robert Norris, a seemingly chance encounter around 2004 at a housing/economic development conference in Oakland, California set his feet on a path to purpose. He was presenting at the conference for Century Housing Corporation. Lula Ballton was presenting for West Angeles Community Development Corporation. They had not seen each other for more than 20 years, not since their days at Los Angeles City College. Robert describes Lula's surprise. "Lula said, 'When I saw your name on the program, I said, God, that can't be,'" because she had long since relegated him to jail or the graveyard. Robert laughs. "I think we ended up funding, from Century Housing, a contract that [WACDC] would do for development."

A few years later, having witnessed Robert's expertise, Lula invited him to join the team at West Angeles CDC. After a year of resistance, "it was like God said, 'You're a hard head, boy. When I'm telling you to go somewhere, you'd better be listening.'" Again, Robert laughs at the recollection. "So, I ended up saying to Lula, 'Yeah, I'm available.'"

Embrace Spiritual Power as a Christian CDC

Robert, who had been working in the private sector, could immediately see the spiritual difference working for the Christian CDC. Raised as a "black Catholic" where the "roles of the Father and Son are very much emphasized," and the "Holy Spirit is understated," Robert was surprised by the "power" of the Holy Spirit that permeated his experience at West Angeles CDC. "There's a joy to working every day" when our job is to "remind people" in practical ways that

God loves them. Robert's daily signature greeting to the WACDC staff was, "Are you ready for the glorious opportunity to serve?"

Robert learned in the Marine Corps that people who believe are more powerful than any weapon. "I could see that being reflected in a lot of the messages that are in faith-based community development." He cites Nehemiah 2:20, the foundational Scripture of the WACDC vision statement: *"We are servants of the God who rules from heaven, and he will make our work succeed. So we will start rebuilding Jerusalem"* (Contemporary English Version).

Foster the Church-CDC Connection

The source of WACDC's vision was West Angeles Church. To keep the vision aligned, both the church and the CDC were intentional about remaining closely connected. The CDC attended the weekly senior staff meetings at West Angeles Church. During those meetings, Lula or Robert kept the church apprised of plans and activities in the CDC and ascertained how the CDCs programs could "tie into" the ministry of the church. West Angeles CDC and West Angeles Church had "a very strong relationship," Robert notes.

Stay Plugged into the Shifting Needs in the Community

The West Angeles vision remained a fixed point, but needs in the community were dynamic. In order to develop, improve, or adjust programs to meet the changing needs, WACDC had to stay plugged into the needs of the community. One means of accomplishing that aim was to become a member (and attend meetings) of the Community Advisory Board of the Community Redevelopment Agency of Los Angeles, a public agency dedicated to revitalizing, refurbishing, and renewing economically underserved areas of Los Angeles by partnering in housing, commercial, neighborhood, and economic development.

In addition, because of the size of West Angeles Church, political leaders invited representatives of West Angeles to come to community forums. "It was a two-way street," Robert says. "These elected representatives made sure to check with West Angeles if they were doing something." All of the ministers in the area also met quarterly to keep communication and knowledge flowing.

Another opportunity for community communication occurred when the CDC was "on the ground" offering their services. They could hear firsthand the issues uppermost in the minds of the people they served. "People would come in and they're talking about, 'I'm losing my home. I can't find a job.'" In fact, in 2011, these and other issues are what WACDC identified in the problem statement of its Crenshaw Revitalization Initiative submitted to the Local Initiatives Support Corporation (LISC), a nonprofit connecting hard-to-tap public and private resources with underinvested places and people working to access opportunities (*www.lisc.org/about-us/*). WACDC was not content, however, "just dealing with homelessness." *For the Crenshaw Revitalization Initiative, WACDC had posed the questions: Where do we see the Crenshaw neighborhood being revitalized? What is that vision? The plan for West Angeles Plaza submitted to LISC was "our vision of what we thought the Crenshaw neighborhood should look like."*

Bring Vision to Life

West Angeles Plaza, a commercial plaza with over 20,000 sq. ft. at the corner of Crenshaw and Jefferson Boulevards in Los Angeles, housed, among other commercial opportunities, Union Bank and Ralph's Supermarket. Ralph's was going to close, causing the community to become what Robert describes as, "essentially a food desert." The initiative to operate and develop West Angeles Plaza would not only create 100 construction jobs and 40 long-term jobs in the community but also "create that separate stream of income that wouldn't make you totally dependent on government or on the kindness of strangers" for the CDC, shifting the paradigm from "We got our hand out" to "No, we own this." Robert expounds, "We can build our own portfolio of properties. The church wouldn't have to take [money] out of the collection if the CDC could have its own separate source of revenue."

The recently approved light rail that would travel down Crenshaw Boulevard from just north of the property to the Los Angeles International Airport would make West Angeles Plaza a valuable property. The initiative included funds to organize community residents to participate in the employment opportunities that the project would provide, improve the physical aesthetics along the route, and revitalize elements of the Crenshaw Corridor along the proposed route. This was all a part of Lula's vision.

Press on to the Higher Call

But the vision was not without opposition. Robert recounts, "There was one group from outside the community that basically protested the West Angeles Plaza every step of the way." West Angeles Plaza "did finally come online and was delivering, but it took an abnormally long time to flourish." Robert ponders why "minority-owned, church-owned, community-controlled projects" face such opposition. He lets the question hang in the air before finally continuing. He concludes that it is "a residue of thinking that community control is not the right of the people in the community. It is that you are to be ministered to as opposed to having your own."

But WACDC's vision of West Angeles Plaza, one that rose into existence from words on the page of an initiative to a brick-and-mortar development on the streets of Los Angeles, and similar visions of Christian CDCs across the country, motivate people of character to contend for the Beloved Community.

Hire Highly Skilled People

One of the best ways to contend for your community as a Christian CDC, Robert advises, is to be prudent in your structure and leadership, and to ensure proper levels of funding. "You don't just want all the board to be very enthusiastic but unskilled." A for-profit business requires people skilled in accounting, legal, and other backgrounds who "believe in the mission" and are "not just going through the motions" to ensure that the business operates legitimately and efficiently. Likewise, a Christian CDC needs highly skilled and committed people and, in addition, people who embrace the fiscal responsibility of fundraising. The board, in particular, must believe that it is their responsibility to make sure that adequate revenues flow into the CDC. In order to get to the level where you can come to the table "not begging" but rather as a "participant" in the proceedings, you must "demonstrate that you are not operating on the edge." Financial partners will want to see three to five years of your financial records to verify that you are not what an accountant would call "an ongoing concern."

In addition to "stable, qualified leadership top to bottom," a CDC must have "adequate staffing resources configured for their activities." If you are doing counseling, then you need an MSW (Master of Social Work degree) or a Ph.D., "someone with the technical certification to do that work." If you are building housing, you need someone who has demonstrated excellence in that field with a stellar reputation.

Robert further cautions that beyond having properly qualified staff, the CDC must be properly resourced. "You can't ask people to always work miracles." That's especially important for a Christian

CDC where the lines between God's faithfulness and our work unto the Lord can get blurred. While a Christian CDC must take care not to work with a slack hand expecting God to perform unnecessary displays of power, neither should the Christian CDC take on more than it should. "I think one of the cautions Lula got from Bishop Blake was not to always step up to solve problems that the government should solve." For example, the Christian CDC cannot be the only organization dealing with homelessness because the government may fund you and then three years later, pull the funding. Then the community is looking to the CDC to solve the problem. "So you have to be really careful about getting involved in certain activities that you cannot sustain."

Advice from the Trenches for Christian CDCs

- Try to anticipate and be prepared for opposition you might find in your community.
- Make sure you develop programs that address a real need in the community rather than those that advance an individual's ambition.
- Encourage your congregation to "build a sustainable circle in the community." Support business owners in the congregation with the resources of the community because they cannot survive the big commercial enterprises who offer lower prices but who take those profits out of the community. It makes a significant difference in the economic health of the community.
- Even though you may be starting small, as you develop programs and partnerships, control as much of the transaction as you can. "Sometimes the biggest money deal isn't the best deal for you." If someone offers you a million dollars, you need to ask yourself if they are getting something out of the deal that is not apparent to you. Are

you giving up more control than you realize? You do not want to become a million-dollar slave. Maintain control.

- Be scrupulous not only about financial transactions but also about transactions that leverage your reputation. Being associated with people of disreputable character or being drawn into a scam is bad for the religious community as well as your Christian CDC.
- Always remember that there is "a third player on the field playing against you" because you are a Christian organization. The battle is not against flesh and blood, so fight your spiritual opposition, but also keep your eyes wide open to the devices of physical opponents.

Robert, still a Marine at heart, does not consider himself "a Bible man" with a thorough knowledge of Scripture. Yet, having just quoted the West Angeles CDC vision scripture, Nehemiah 2:20, he proceeds to cite Hosea 4:6, *"My people are destroyed for lack of knowledge,"* and Isaiah 54:17, *"No weapon formed against me shall prosper,"* as "the undercurrent of a lot of [WACDC] programs." Robert notes, "I think all I did was go after opportunities and look for opportunities to tie into that vision, mostly from secular sources." Maintaining the vision as the North Star, Robert did not have to "quote the Bible to put its intent" into everything he did at West Angeles CDC. He is a strategist who brought skill and competence to the table, knowing that the God who rules from heaven would make the work succeed.

> ***People who believe are more powerful than any weapon.***

TUNUA THRASH-NTUK

Executive Director

2010 – 2015

Tunua Thrash-Ntuk grew up in her grandmother's house steeped in a philosophy of hospitality and service to others. Her grandmother was president of the usher board, the highest role a woman could have in their very traditional church. To Tunua, the ushers epitomized hospitality. "The usher is the first person you see, they welcome you in, they begin to create and set up for you the experience of what you're going to have there within church." Tunua wanted to do whatever her beloved role model was doing. "Of course, I was on the junior usher board." Thus began a commitment to serving others that would define the trajectory of Tunua's life. Her goal became to get the best education she could and come back to support the people in the community.

Early in 2010, when Tunua was a fellow at the Greenlining Institute—a statewide public policy organization that brings together a coalition of civic, business, and faith-based leaders to ensure that low-income and minority communities have access to capital to help them achieve great things in their neighborhoods—she met Lula Ballton. Dr. Ballton was a Board member of the Greenlining Institute. After graduating from MIT, Tunua contacted Lula and was hired to work at West Angeles CDC as a project manager to assist with WACDC's first commercial real estate project, the development of West Angeles Plaza. So began her career in community service, a vision for which she had been preparing all her life.

Commit to Your Vision

In the same way that Tunua was committed to her personal vision, a CDC must be committed to theirs. "Your programs come and go, but your vision should still be describing what it is that you are doing no matter what the program is," Tunua says. At WACDC, the vision is "really all about creating the beloved community." The vision does not expressly state that one has to have a house, "but most would agree that having a decent, safe, affordable home would be replicating the beloved community." The vision doesn't state that there is no violence, but most would agree that a beloved community is one where you can live in safety, free from a "war-like" state. The vision does not state that one has to have a job, but a beloved community is one in which people have the income to meet their needs. Being able to access these things is "what creating the beloved community is all about."

WACDC holds fast to their vision, even in the midst of opposition, and that's what makes their programs so effective. The homeownership programs, for example, focus both on moving people into homeownership and maintaining homeownership. "As a staff, as a team, we were committed to the larger concept of how do we build wealth in this community, and building wealth means that people need to be able to buy into the American dream and be part of that." Most lenders and realtors viewed WACDC's clients as people who would never be able to buy a home. "We just didn't take that perspective," Tunua asserts. "It didn't matter if you walked in and you had income at a certain level." WACDC helped their clients create financial plans that enabled them to invest and begin building wealth, and then connected them to down payment programs. The CDC encouraged clients to have faith, and to act on that faith by seeking better jobs because "we believe as people of faith that you deserve this; it's coming to you, so you've got to be ready when that next job comes," Tunua reflects. "We were very good at that and we brought lenders and realtors around us who also believed in that and saw our clients as the next homeowner."

So, according to Tunua, your vision and your mission are vitally important because if you are following them correctly, everything flows from them. In the case of WACDC, each time they decide on a new program they consider how it would contribute to the beloved community in a way that, perhaps, no other organization is doing or that is synergistic with existing programs.

Ensure the Board Commits to Funding

Board members must also be committed to the vision of the CDC. For Christian CDCs, Tunua explains, the board should also understand and believe in the connection between the church and the faith-based mission. It is especially important for a newly formed organization that wants to stay close to its faith roots to have as many Christian board members as possible. As the Christian CDC gets older and established and has created "some institutional history and knowledge" that becomes ingrained in the culture of the organization, the CDC can determine if it is beneficial to invite a board member from a different church or religion—or even to "step on the wild side and identify someone who's not religious in any way." But the CDC should give careful consideration to what the non-Christian candidate brings to the organization that is so compelling that it warrants them a seat at the table.

Beyond embracing the faith-based nature of the Christian CDC, one of the most vital contributions that the board offers, especially to a new CDC, is funding. "Starting out, the board definitely needs to be giving at 100 percent," Tunua declares. "Not that everybody has to give a million dollars, but everybody needs to give something" and work toward what they can comfortably give or raise.

Next, the board should build the community of donors through fundraising. West Angeles CDC hosts an annual gala as a means to identify individuals and organizations who believe in their vision. Each board member is responsible to give or raise $4,000 to pay for the event, positioning the CDC to secure funds beyond the event costs. WACDC brings Christian organizations, corporations, small businesses, and foundations together for one annual event, creating a built-in set of donors who look forward every year to "coming out and celebrating the successes" of a ministry they believe in. Tunua cautions CDCs, however, to be reasonable with the budget, especially the first time hosting such an event. "You don't want to spend all your money throwing the party and then you don't have anything to show for it."

Tunua urges new CDCs to understand that they will have to "rely on friends of the ministry before they can get institutional supporters." A major foundation or corporation will not fund you until you can demonstrate that you have gotten targeted outcomes in the community. Larger institutions are looking for what you have done with what you have. "Many of them cannot fund start-up nonprofits, and many of them require several years of audited financials, and that costs money" to pay auditors. A start-up CDC should not think that by opening their doors, "the big $50,000, $100,000, $200,000 [donation] is coming. It's not likely to come, unless you know an individual who can give like that."

Delve into the Data

Tunua explains that donations and audit trails are only part of the picture of a CDC's overall health. In the for-profit sector, the evaluation methods of success in the business world are aligned to financial statements. While financials are important in the nonprofit world, there is the "other element of qualitative and even quantitative outcome that you might look at in a nonprofit organization." Success at WACDC, for example, is not based on invoices per month, but on how many people got a new home, were those homes safe, how many homes were saved, or how many new jobs were created.

Tunua advises a CDC to delve even deeper into the data. Ask, now that this person has a home, what does that mean? "What are the additional benefits that we can evaluate or try to support so that we better understand the totality of the impact?" By asking these questions, Tunua says, WACDC became "even more sophisticated in how we evaluate the impact we're having." Data became knowledge.

Seek Partners Who Share Knowledge

Tunua strongly believes that knowledge acquisition must be an ongoing part of a successful CDC. She recommends that a CDC, to the extent that it can, start with professionals trained in the specific staff role or program area for which they will be responsible, but that is just the beginning. In her own case, Tunua realized she needed "on-the-ground experience and additional training" to make the real estate development project successful. Tunua did more than take applicable training that was available to her. "I was thoughtful about bringing on consultants who were more experienced than I was, and then I learned. I used that as a way to fill any knowledge gaps I had."

Further, when opportunities arose to work with other organizations, Tunua was strategic about increasing the accumulated knowledge of the CDC. "Not every organization doing real estate development was willing to teach us or to allow for the knowledge transfer. A lot of those organizations wanted to keep that knowledge, but I specifically chose organizations and people at those institutions who believed in knowledge transfer." With that strategy,

Tunua was able to effectively move the real estate agenda for West Angeles CDC forward.

Explore New Ideas to Expand

When Tunua accepted the executive director helm after Lula retired from West Angeles CDC in 2013, she was resolved that "this would not be a maintenance program." Tunua wanted to do more than they had previously done. She wanted to expand. She wanted to invest in some of the older real estate assets and do something different with them. She wanted to buy things they had not bought before and activate existing assets. Tunua explains her concept of the role. "Being an executive director means you've got to manage the people, and you've got to bring in the resources. You've got to manage those resources as they come in." She continues, "But all of that begins with a vision for what is possible."

Under Tunua's leadership, West Angeles CDC expanded their housing programs. The CDC started redevelopment plans on a number of older projects so that the CDC could not only benefit financially from them but also improve the units for the families. The timing was right in the capital history of the developments to be able to leverage the equity and do more with them. WACDC also opened up a separate office to handle the West Coast operations for Fannie Mae and Freddie Mac to help people save their homes, becoming the number one provider of mortgage support for people who were experiencing trouble paying the mortgage or maintaining their home. WACDC had the West Coast national grants, covering Hawaii to the Midwest.

WACDC expanded its economic development to include a small business loan fund. Tunua recounts, "I had been able to work with a bank and get micro dollars from them—a couple hundred thousand dollars—that we could then target to local small businesses." Though Tunua did not know how to do small-business lending, using her knowledge-transfer strategy, she identified a partner who was willing to share knowledge, which allowed the CDC to begin to develop their expertise internally. Tunua is particularly proud of her program to "work with young boys of color, in particular young black boys, in the neighborhood to intervene in their lives so that they were put on a new path toward restoration and employment and finishing their education."

Maximize Volunteer Performance

In addition to visionary leadership, the achievements Tunua describes required a strong team. To augment human resources, Tunua focused on maximizing volunteer performance. She offers this advice to CDCs: "Once you've assessed their skills, try to properly identify an assignment that fits their interests." If they are not interested, they will not do as good of a job. Even if they do not have a lot of expertise in an area, if they are interested, they are likely to have the enthusiasm to learn."

To ensure that volunteers had a supervisor to whom they could turn for support, Tunua set finite periods for volunteer stints of 60 or 90 days. At the end of the period, there was a checkpoint to see if the supervisor and the volunteer mutually agreed to continue or end the engagement. These clear checkpoints help to keep volunteers motivated for the length of the assignment.

Tunua also made sure that a volunteer's work was reviewed before it left the CDC. A volunteer could "produce something" that could be "added to something that was going out the door, but what they produced will not be the final product. I spent a lot of time watching things."

Recruit Young Christian Volunteers with Leadership Potential

In an effort to recruit volunteers, Tunua did an internship program with Biola University, a Christian school in La Mirada, California. "Doing an internship at an institution like that allows you to find young people who are motivated, excited, and on fire for the ministry that you are developing." They may also have ideas about how to advance the ministry in new ways. Tunua also used the internship program as a staff recruiting method for young Christian leaders who are interested in nonprofit work.

Another opportunity to recruit Christian volunteers with leadership potential is in the church. "Stay in touch with the young people in your church as they go off to school," Tunua says. "There are young folks who are looking for internships or want a job when they get home, like I did. Encourage and create the space for them to know that there is a place for them when they come back to the community."

Tunua also did internships with people in the church who were "in between opportunities." She assessed them and found a division in the CDC to which they could contribute for a period of time. The "formality of making it an internship" versus simply volunteer work gave them something more valuable to put on their resume because it's a formal program. "West Angeles was such a large church; there were a lot of talented people."

Invite Young People to the Table

One of Tunua's biggest challenges as a young executive director was building consensus to move past the paradigms of some of her older peers on the board. "I was very ready to think about what a Christian community development strategy looks like for the 21st century and beyond. And I didn't have as many people on my board who were of that age or had that experience. And so I feel like some of the things that I was ready to talk about, the board wasn't quite there." She perceived that one of the biggest threats to West Angeles CDC was what would happen in the absence of Bishop Blake. "How does the organization maintain itself?" she asks. "What happens when a number of the older saints are no longer there?"

She wrestled with other questions. "How are we engaging young people, young professionals, in the ministry and the CDC? What does my generation need and want differently from the previous generation? How do we do more?" Tunua felt that the CDC could do even more to connect its work with the ministry. "My generation sees fluidity between loving the earth and loving God, for example." Some believe that because you see a connection between the two, you are espousing a different religion. "So as an institution, as a Christian institution, we've got to think about how are we reaching those people so that they can continue to view the pews and the work and the ministry and the fellowship in ways that are not just about sitting in church on Sunday" but more in line with "today's national and local realities."

When asked what has made West Angeles CDC so venerable, Tunua responds, "the relationship to the church itself; it's very strong. And Bishop Blake is a dynamic and a well-regarded leader. He's a great leader that has been able to spin off and create and invest in this other entity." WACDC also has a founder like Lula "who is dynamic in her own right and very engaging and compelling and committed to this work." She has created a big reputation for the organization. WACDC's leaders are captivating and desire to be with people, whereas some other ministries might be "just a little more closed off."

Tunua adds that WACDC has also cultivated a culture of

growth. Ever with an eye to the future, Tunua is also cognizant that West Angeles CDC must continue to grow as an institution whose reputation is based not on its dynamic leaders but rather on the people it serves.

ECONOMIC DEVELOPMENT DEPARTMENT

The Economic Development Department strives to serve as a catalyst in the creation of living-wage jobs, stronger businesses, and state-of-the-art commercial properties that will create momentum for ongoing improvements in the lives of people who live and work in the Crenshaw District and in the surrounding communities of South Los Angeles.

Our three core service areas are Commercial Real Estate Development, Small Business Assistance, and Small Business Development. The Economic Development Department focuses on projects that will result in sustainable change and inspire private-sector investment.

COMMERCIAL REAL ESTATE DEVELOPMENT: The Economic Development Department aims to reverse the trend of disinvestment in inner-city commercial districts by redeveloping strategic parcels into state-of-the-art office, retail, industrial, or mixed-use developments.

The Economic Development Department has an active roster of potential sites for commercial and/or mixed-use redevelopment. The Department has proven experience in identifying and securing sites, coordinating predevelopment assessments, and preparing finance packages for commercial real estate projects.

Our expertise in the following areas has contributed to our role as faith-based economic development industry leaders:

- Identifying and securing sites for commercial (retail, office, industrial, mixed-use facilities construction)
- Identifying and packaging financing for commercial real estate project development
- Coordinating all public and environmental reviews and architecture and design
- Attracting businesses to either invest or lease space in new developments.

Our Entrepreneur Training Program provides eight weeks of intensive instruction on the opportunities and challenges of owning a business. Building on each lesson, students complete weekly assignments, and by the end of the course, each student has created a viable business plan. Participants also receive individual hours of technical assistance from experienced industry practitioners.

SMALL BUSINESS ASSISTANCE: a program of the Economic Development Department that trains neighborhood entrepreneurs in the basics of starting and operating a successful small business. Small Business Assistance conducts individual technical assistance and follow-up to help entrepreneurs strengthen their finances, marketing, and operation. The Small Business Community Power Breakfast series provides pertinent topics of interest to local business owners each quarter. Example topics include:

- Small Business Credit
- Marketing and Growth Opportunities
- Procurement Opportunities

SMALL BUSINESS DEVELOPMENT: West Angeles CDC has identified three sectors of the economy ripe for exploration of business opportunities that will create and eventually sustain large labor markets of above minimum-wage jobs. The three sectors include the energy, food, and health industries. These industries represent:

- Fast-growing fields
- Fields of constant innovation and technology improvement
- Labor intensive fields
- Fields that will result in cost reduction opportunities for low- to moderate-income communities
- Fields that will result in health improvement opportunities for low- to moderate-income communities

The Economic Development Department works with individuals and institutions with cutting-edge ideas in the target industry sectors. The Department specifically supports such ventures by:

- Utilizing the resources of the inner-city community to beta test markets, products, and services
- Fostering innovative ideas and shaping the business planning exercise
- Conducting research to better understand market opportunities and consumer responses

PAUL TURNER

Director of Economic Development
1994 – 1998

It started with a conversation.

Paul Turner came to work with Lula Ballton at the Union Rescue Mission in Los Angeles in 1993, where he served as the Coordinator for Community Development. She was the Director of the Education department. Friend and colleague Grant Power introduced them and recommended she hire Paul to work on their team. After a few months, Lula was leaving the Mission to become the new head of social services and outreach ministries at West Angeles Church. The conversation that would impact the lives of so many people took place primarily between Lula and Grant Power.

Grant said, "West Angeles should have a community development corporation."

Lula said, "What's that and how does it differ from general church outreach?"

Lula listened intently as Grant explained the concept. As an attorney with a background in economic justice and civil rights, Lula knew immediately that the vehicle of a community development corporation would be the ideal framework for the goals she wanted to accomplish in the community. She presented the idea to Bishop Blake, the wise, charismatic leader of West Angeles Church. Liking the concept, Bishop Blake gave his approval, suggesting that Lula should run it. Lula returned to Paul and Grant, and said, "Okay, you guys got me into this; now you've got to help me put this together."

Shortly thereafter, at the end of 1993, Paul left the Mission to help Lula with West Angeles Community Development Corporation. He assisted with setting it up; working with the bishop, Lula, and Grant in writing the mission statement; getting board members willing to give of their time, talent, and treasure; and securing some of the early funding. Grant Power was also hired at the new CDC, primarily writing grants.

Stay on Mission

Paul describes a community development corporation as "a community empowerment exercise where people come together and make a decision that they want to impact change in their community." Once that decision is made, you must arm yourself to fulfill your mission. The mission is foremost. At the top of the organizational chart is the mission statement. Under the mission statement is the board. Under the board are the executives followed by staff and volunteers. Paul is emphatic: "The mission statement is what guides the entire organization. It's like our constitution. If it's not about our mission, then we don't do it."

A community development corporation must be clear about its mission, and that mission is based on a vision. Paul describes Bishop Blake as the "spiritual visionary" for everything at West Angeles Church and by extension, the CDC, as evidenced by his quick grasp of Lula's vision for the community development corporation concept and his resolve to take immediate action. Bishop Blake has always been intentional in his assertion that, though legally separate entities, the community development corporation of a church works within the greater vision and ministry of the church, allowing the church to accomplish community-impact ministry it could not otherwise do and form partnerships it would not otherwise have.

Paul stresses the importance for any church engaged in community development work to understand that successful community impact is not about what's good for the church, but about what's good for the community. One of the community needs that West

Angeles CDC wanted to impact was affordable housing. Many CDCs at the time focused on housing development, but the scope of WACDC's mission entailed a more comprehensive approach, addressing business development, job creation, and social services, in its desire to meet what Paul describes as "a panoply of needs."

Leverage the Unexpected

No sooner had WACDC begun to implement its mission, becoming the hands and feet of Jesus to the community, when on Monday, January 17, 1994, which was the Martin Luther King holiday and Paul's first day on the job, the Northridge Earthquake struck Los Angeles. The 6.7-magnitude earthquake killed over 60 people, injured more than 9,000, and caused widespread damage throughout the city. The Santa Monica Freeway collapsed less than a mile from West Angeles Church. Many houses were knocked off their foundations, and buildings were red-tagged uninhabitable or "seismically deficient."

West Angeles CDC launched into action to address the needs of the community after the catastrophe. The CDC obtained a city contract to do earthquake response work, and it was the focus of the first year. Displaced people needed housing. Many people with damaged homes needed assistance applying for FEMA loans, obtaining home equity lines of credit, and dealing with their insurance companies. The CDC's earthquake response efforts—working with the community, elected officials, financiers, and the financial services community—made them a "credible player" in the community.

Boldly Solicit Funding

After the initial earthquake response, Paul focused on organizational development and, in conjunction with Lula, relationship development. He recounts a time when he gave an elevator speech while actually in an elevator. He was attending a meeting in downtown Los Angeles with city councilman Mark Ridley Thomas, who was chair of the city's economic development committee. The vice president of Bank of America was there attending another meeting. Afterward, he and Paul shared an elevator. "He shook my hand and introduced himself. I introduced myself. I said, 'Yes, I've been wanting to talk with you guys about a meeting with someone at your foundation.' He said, 'You should talk to the president of our foundation.' I said, 'Oh, can I use your name?' He says, 'Sure, no problem at all.'

"As soon as I got back to the office, I contacted her. She said, 'I would love to talk with you. I've been wanting to learn more about what you guys are doing.' So we had her come to the church, met in the boardroom, talked, and that's when we got our first major grant...for $25,000." WACDC then received federal grants. Leveraging the name of one bank and foundation better positioned the CDC to acquire funding from other institutions. Developing relationships, confidently and professionally seizing opportunities, and acting quickly and decisively in alignment with missional objectives are all factors contributing to the success of West Angeles CDC.

Seek Civic Involvement

Another factor contributing to the long-term impact of West Angeles CDC is civic involvement. WACDC was introduced to what Paul calls, with obvious admiration, an "upstart organization from up north" called the Greenlining Coalition. The Greenlining Coalition, an organization of minority associations whose mission is to advance economic opportunity and empowerment for people of color through advocacy, community and coalition building, research, and leadership development, was formed as the solution to redlining (a process by which banks and other institutions refuse to offer mortgages or offer worse rates to customers in certain neigh-borhoods based on their racial and ethnic composition (*https://www. thoughtco.com/redlining-definition-4157858*).

West Angeles CDC was the first faith-based organization extend-ed an invitation to join the Greenlining Coalition. Lula became a board member and represented the faith community. Through this alliance, WACDC got involved on the ground floor of a negotiation process to convince Wells Fargo, a California bank, to make a sizable financial commitment in its community development and commu-nity investment activities in the State of California. In return, the Coalition would testify on Wells Fargo's behalf before the Federal Reserve Board to be approved to take over First Interstate Bank, the only major bank headquartered in Los Angeles.

In 1995, Wells Fargo came to the table with the very sizable commitment of $45 billion over 10 years, at the time, one of the biggest commitments of its type ever made, much of it targeted to affordable housing, small business development, and charitable contributions. The Coalition testified that because of Wells Fargo's commitment to the community, the Federal Reserve Board should approve them over their out-of-state competitor, the Bank of Min-nesota. Wells Fargo was approved, and other banks followed suit. This favorable outcome for the community established the influ-ence of West Angeles CDC, and Wells Fargo became one of WAC-DC's biggest financial-institution partners.

In addition to many other multifaceted benefits, *Paul makes a case for the critical role of civic involvement partly "because, without the advocacy and activism, we wouldn't have had the funding opportunities we had.* Advocacy was always a part of our mission as well. So it's not like we were standing on the side here saying, 'Oh, somebody help us.' No, we were out there in people's faces. We were picketing, we were protesting, we were showing up at hearings." West Angeles CDC took CEOs to task, compelling them to come to the table.

Seek Seasoned Mentors

WACDC's organizational and civic expertise was not developed in a vacuum. While there is a significant responsibility to educate yourself, Paul says, "We got advice. We sought it. We solicited it. We loved the advice where we didn't know what we were doing, and so we really had some mentors in this process." One such mentor was Jacquelyn "Jackie" Dupont-Walker of Ward A.M.E. Church in Los Angeles, founding president of Ward Economic Development Corporation. "She had already built senior housing, so she already knew this stuff. She was and still is a community pioneer person to be reckoned with. She was our guru, our mother."

Another mentor was "the late and wonderful" Marva Smith Battle-Bey, Executive Director of Vermont Slauson Economic Development Corporation. In addition to being instrumental in the California Reinvestment Coalition, she knew a lot about the history of community development in South Los Angeles, the State of California, and the country because she served on the board of the National Community Reinvestment Coalition (NCRC). Formed in 1990 to increase the flow of private capital into traditionally underserved communities, the NCRC is an association of more than 600 community-based organizations that promote access to basic banking services, affordable housing, entrepreneurship, job creation, and vibrant communities. With her extensive knowledge and experience, Smith Battle-Bey created a commercial real estate development and building training program with the City of Los Angeles and the University of Southern California. "She had me go through that training so we could learn how to do commercial real estate development, not just housing," notes Paul.

"We had a lot of mentors, advisors, people that we went to. We sought advice in the community and the church." Paul reiterates this important key to WACDC's success. In addition, the Christian

Community Development Association was an invaluable resource. CDCs can look to their own local resources to find seasoned mentors like Dupont-Walker and Smith Battle-Bey. In smaller communities where there may be an apparent scarcity of qualified advisors, CDCs can mine regional resources and conferences for prospective mentors.

Be the Expert on Your Community

West Angeles CDC leveraged and augmented its legacy of accumulated expertise from mentors to become even more deeply involved in the community and increase its long-term impact. For example, WACDC played a large role in the Community Reinvestment Agency of Los Angeles, whose goal was to revitalize commercial corridors throughout LA. WACDC was part of the project area committee planning. "We lent capacity to other long-term planning goals in the city. That's important," remarks Paul.

WACDC was well received by the city council and played a big role in helping to change laws and legislation. Testifying before state, local, and federal committees about legislation, the CDC was very much a part of making new law. "If you're not at the table, you're on the menu," says Paul. "Not only do you have to know what's going on, but you have to make sure it can't go on without you."

A practical way to get a seat at the table is to become the expert on your community. "Get information on your community that no one else has, and then trade that information. Don't give it away." WACDC worked with a small business development center that did a demographic study based upon 1990 census data within the boundaries of the CDC's service area. This provided WACDC with a valuable volume of data to demonstrate that it knew its community. "I could go into a meeting, and I could tell people, 'Well, you know, 59 percent of our neighborhood rents; 41 percent are homeowners,' based on that demographic. So that was very important. That was very useful at the very beginning because I could pull that data and use it in grant proposals or speeches or in conversations to make new relationships."

West Angeles CDC also used the demographic data to not only assess the needs in the community but equally important, to perform asset assessment. WACDC valued ABCD, asset-based community development, which asked the questions: What are the assets in our community? How do you build on those assets? The answers might identify the industries in the community that needed support and industry clusters that could work together. For example, the CDC facilitated a new association for a cluster of African-American real estate developers to come together over a monthly breakfast to discuss real estate development in the community, ensuring that the city and the Community Reinvestment Agency were involved and focused on blighted areas where development needed to occur. Another application of ABCD would allow a CDC to enumerate, for example, and leverage the number of beauty shops and barber-shops in their community, a viable part of the billion-dollar black hair care industry.

Understand the Christian Distinction

In addition to being an expert in the community and in civic matters, a Christian community development corporation must recognize its biblical mandate to live out the unconditional love of God through the person of Jesus Christ. The Christian CDC is ultimately an expression of faith, a tangible and impactful outworking of faith in the community because faith without works is dead. It is essential that board members, Christian or otherwise, respect the spiritual mission of the Christian CDC.

A Christian CDC is often directly associated with a church that helps shoulder spiritual and, especially initially, financial responsibility. Lula Ballton's initial position was to be the Social Services Director of West Angeles Church. After West Angeles embraced the concept of the community development corporation, social services were brought under the CDC. The church was still a place where people in the community could go for assistance, but it was delivered by the CDC. WACDC met emergency needs daily, assisting those who needed bus tokens, funeral expenses, rental assistance, mortgage assistance, shelter, and protection from abusive environments.

Though WACDC eventually garnered city contracts for rental assistance, initially these emergency services were all funded by the church. The church allocated the funds for emergency services that the CDC administered. Churches desiring to start a CDC as a way to procure outside funding should understand two things: a CDC must first be part of the vision, mission, and values of the church; and the church must give sacrificially to finance the initial efforts of the CDC. West Angeles, a prosperous and generous church, because of their belief in the mission of the CDC and their understanding that the CDC was part of their ministry, wrote a $20,000 check that paid for the early staff when the CDC had no money; and they continued to do that for years. The church also provided funds to purchase property for the first housing project. West Angeles Church subsidized the CDC until it became self-sufficient, which was in the CDC's expansion stage.

Know Your Capacity and Partner with Others

A Christian CDC's relationship to the church should inspire it to be moved by compassion and do what God is saying. "If we see the homeless people in front of the church during the week," Paul wonders, "are we just going to run them off? Are we going to do something about it? Is God calling us to do something? Are you going to just continue to call the police?" Assistance might mean the youth making sandwiches to distribute under supervision. Or is the church called to do something greater than give out sandwiches? It's a capacity issue.

At one point, a small church planning renovations approached Paul for advice about their desire to install a shower for the homeless. "I said, 'Well, that all sounds very nice, but do you really have the capacity to do that?" Providing assistance, in this case, is more complex than simply installing a shower. The church would need to develop a complete program with linkages to other services. Clinical experts would need to be available because most of the people who are homeless are not just in need of a shower; they are mentally ill or struggling with other issues. The church would need to be equipped to handle case management.

The desire to help is born out of compassion and is a laudable first step. But proposed solutions must be carefully thought through. If your church has the capacity and is called to proceed, link up with another organization, Los Angeles County Housing Homeless Services Agency, for example, to have a memorandum of understanding where they can, perhaps, come two days a week when the showers are open to provide referrals to other county services. Collaboration is the key to leveraging other services that are already funded and seeking impactful links within the community. Linking with other groups, agencies, and departments, whenever feasible, can help those organizations to be more efficient as well through your activities. These mutually beneficial collaborations increase the power, influence, and prestige of the CDC in the community.

Start Small

A church planning to start a CDC should recognize that influence in the community is not gained immediately; it takes time and commitment. Be in prayer and study, Paul recommends. Search the Scriptures and use discernment to obtain clarity about what God is calling you to do. "You don't have to start out big. Start out small," he advises. It may be best to start with a seed project before attempting a CDC. He recommends the book *If Jesus Were Mayor: How God Can Use Your Church to Transform Your Community* by Bob Moffitt and Karla Tesch, which discusses what a smaller congregation can do to impact their community.

Perhaps a laundromat needs to be cleaned, or a liquor store needs to be shut down because there are too many in the community. It could be a beautification project of the corner down the street from the church or of a rundown bus stop. Seed projects are small projects that can be accomplished with local resources in days, weeks, or months rather than years.

In the case of the hypothetical bus stop beautification, you would talk to the passengers at the bus stop and elicit feedback about the trash on the ground, the lack of a waste bin, the dilapidated bench, the lack of shade, and so on. You let riders know that your church intends to help change the condition of the bus stop. You plan it out and obtain volunteer support, gather signatures, attend transit authority meetings, get the attention of your city council. Perhaps your councilman helps out. They assign a person to work with you because of your church's organization and commitment. With their partnership, you achieve your goal of a beautified bus stop. You have a ribbon-cutting ceremony, inviting the community, the city council, the press, and the transit authority. You all celebrate together as a community because you have made an impact for positive change. Your influence in the community has begun.

The community is not the only thing that will be impacted—you too will be transformed. When asked how his work with West Angeles CDC impacted him, Paul declares with a pensive laugh, "Oh gosh, I wouldn't be where I am today. It's...everything I've learned, everything I've done...everything. It was my career-defining experience."

> *The Christian CDC is ultimately an expression of faith, a tangible and impactful outworking of faith in the community because faith without works is dead.*

SAMUEL K. HUGHES

Economic Development Manager
1997 – 2001

In 1997, Lula Ballton spotted Sam Hughes at West Angeles Church of God In Christ, where they both attended, and asked him if he had any interest in working with her at West Angeles CDC. That was not the first time Lula Ballton had approached Sam with a challenging assignment. Sitting at the conference table in his spacious office overlooking the City of Los Angeles, Sam smiles. "Lula was my junior high school teacher." As a youth, Sam attended West Angeles Christian Academy. "That's where I initially met her. As I matured, she kept her eye on me. And interestingly enough, when she was at law school at UCLA, I was there as an undergrad at the same time."

Ultimately, Sam carved out a career in finance, loan, and real estate businesses. "I believe [Dr. Ballton] viewed my background, coupled with her impression of me, as viable assets to the CDC. I could bring quantitative and analytical skills to the table, and she trusted me."

"I don't know," Sam replied to Dr. Ballton that morning in church after she invited him to work at WACDC. Undaunted, Lula shared her vision and what she thought Sam could bring to the team as the Economic Development Manager. West Angeles CDC had recently received a grant from Wells Fargo Bank predicated on the CDC's vision to expand business opportunities and bring more jobs into the community. Part of the grant was allocated to hiring someone to assist with economic development, more specifically, business development. "After giving it some consideration," Sam recounts, "I said that I would assist."

Understand the Quid Pro Quo

When Sam started at WACDC, the grant money for economic development was there, but the implementation strategy had not yet been created. "Wells Fargo's funding and expectation were based on the framework of [West Angeles CDC's] vision," Sam notes. "I had to devise a strategy based on the vision of the CDC and the consideration due the grant money from Wells Fargo. We got the money, but Wells Fargo had some expectations. And by the way, Wells Fargo's expectation ultimately was to make certain they could open up as many business accounts as they could. That's the quid pro quo. And I get it; that's what they wanted. Certainly, businesses weren't necessarily focused on switching bank accounts. So, while I was keenly aware of the bank's expectations, I was not trying to force that on any business."

Sam asserts that in order to acquire and maintain mutually beneficial funding relationships, it is important for the CDC to understand the quid pro quo (what the funding partner desires from the relationship), but it is also vital that the CDC remains cognizant of why it exists. Sam expounds, "I'm aware of certain organizations that will chase the money without giving consideration to why they've been established. If someone is offering half a million dollars to anyone that wants to, say, teach kids how to write, a CDC should not just say, 'Let's get it!' and then try to reshape their [articles of incorporation] and their purpose to meet the particular purpose of that grant. So on the one hand, I don't think community development corporations should compromise the intent and purpose of their establishment, but for those that can identify funding sources that complement what they're about, it makes things a lot easier. So you're not doing something just to get a dollar, but you're doing something consistent with who you are, with your vision. Now you're likely to have a partner and a relationship that is sustainable."

Sam maintains that ultimately, sustainable partnerships are about relationships. "It's good to have supporters who have an affinity for a particular organization and care about the mission of the organization. I think there are many supporters or donors that do it in the name of support, and they do not expect anything. I think there are other donors or supporters that do have some anticipation of something. Either way, I think it's important to cultivate relationships. It's important to maintain relationships. Relationships matter in almost any affair, including the space of community development because it's through relationships that you really touch lives."

Evolve Your Program

At WACDC, Sam was initially tasked with "providing technical assistance to businesses, helping them package loans, helping them understand the business plan, and things of that sort." Sam explains his role. "I assessed the community needs relative to one of our ultimate goals: helping to create jobs. Basically, the objective was to assist startup and existing businesses to grow and hire people. So it was really twofold: it was helping businesses and then creating jobs. The presumption is that as businesses thrive, they grow; they expand and may hire. That was the framework of the economic development department." Sam was principally charged with reaching out to the business community. "First, I went to the chambers of commerce and the like to get a pulse on what was happening in the community. Then I literally just went to businesses and inquired, 'Hey, what do you need? What are you doing? How can we help? Free of charge of course.'"

Community development was new to Sam, not in concept, but in practice, so he was "learning on the fly" because he had to "hit the ground running." As a result, program development was an iterative process of listening carefully to clients and adapting to their specific needs. By way of example, Sam recounts his interaction with the owner of a hamburger restaurant. "As I was there observing, I asked the cost of making a burger. The owner didn't know. I said, 'Well, how much does the meat cost?' She told me the wholesale cost of what she paid in bulk, but she hadn't broken it down. I said, 'So that bun, how much does it cost? And how much does it cost to wrap that burger? How much are you actually making on each burger? And the waste, how much do you throw out?' She didn't quite know. So talking with her, I realized some people are entrepreneurial-minded but not necessarily business-minded."

Sam knew that if business owners were to survive and thrive they needed to understand "these nuances" about their businesses. "So as I started to realize that as much as these business owners knew, there were important things they didn't know, I thought maybe I could bring value. I thought we could turn up our offering a notch by creating a toolkit, material that was broadly applicable across a spectrum of businesses." Creating a business plan, for example, was a customized solution for a single business owner. A toolkit, however, could be used by unlimited business owners across a variety of businesses: a flower shop, a restaurant, a hairstylist, and other business. "The toolkit was designed to help an owner have a sustainable business based on what I discovered from watching and learning and listening more than talking. It evolved over time."

Build Wealth for the Community and the CDC

Another program Sam created to promote economic development in the community was a single-family residential homeownership program, wherein "the City or the CDC would purchase properties, distressed properties, foreclosed properties from HUD (Housing and Urban Development Department) to renovate and sell the properties, making them available to first-time homebuyers." Until that point, WACDC had only done apartment deals for rental properties.

Sam desired to help provide the wealth-building power of homeownership to people in the community. "There are benefits to them as a result of being a homeowner, aside from just having a roof over their head. Aside from the equity, the loan interest and property taxes are tax-deductible, so they end up with more money in their pockets. With our financial literacy training, we helped people understand that a home can actually be an investment. Over time, one could leverage the equity to create a decent net worth, buy other properties, and even start a business. In other words, one could tap into the home equity to buy other income-producing, wealth-building assets, rather than tapping into it to buy a car that will only depreciate. It's about understanding the economics."

In his never-ending quest to add value, Sam would ask clients if they would rather save for something lasting or fleeting. "I have since come to refer to it as guns and butter. Butter might look good and taste good, but it melts. Guns are made of metal; they protect you, and they last. Save for tangible assets that appreciate, for example, residential properties, apartment buildings, stocks, etc. They have an impact—they protect you, versus the nice stuff that feels good for a moment or a season." Sam asserts that understanding leverage in the context of homeownership is key to building wealth because most small businesses, still the backbone of the US economy, get started that way. "That's why it means a lot to me that I helped bring about the single-family property disposition program."

The single-family homeownership program also helped to fund WACDC through development fees. Sam describes the process. "Hypothetically, we buy a property for $100,000. We put in $30,000 and sell it for $180,000. That's a $50,000 spread, less any additional contributions to help the buyer get in and our cost of capital or things of that sort. And so while it was to provide a benefit to folks and get them into homes and to have a sustainable program, it brought cash into the CDC to help underwrite other administrative costs. A CDC should keep in mind that it wants to be sustainable. It doesn't want to rely on third-party foundations, banks, or anybody to continue to have to write the check. The upside of real estate development in general, particularly large deals, if they're done right, is that basically, it's an annuity. You continue to get money on a monthly or quarterly or annual basis. This is discretionary money that goes into the general fund, if you will, of the organization to pay staff costs, salaries, rent, leases, any number of different things. Without that, you're constantly on a corner with your hand out asking for money."

The initial funding WACDC used to purchase the properties from HUD came through relationships Sam developed from his background in finance. "I was able to connect the CDC with a private funder that not only would provide capital for the acquisition, but also set aside money for renovation and we would capitalize the payments. For example, if you borrow $100,000 for the acquisition and $30,000 for the construction, you've got a $130,000 loan. Then you need maybe four to six months of construction time. During that time the loan still needs to be paid. What a lender can do is capitalize the interest whereby you borrow more than what you need. You borrow more than just $130,000 for acquisition and construction. Hypothetically, if you've got six months of interest, and let's say it's about a $1,000 payment a month, you need another $6,000 to service the debt while the property is being renovated. So, hypothetically, you might get a loan for $136,000.

"There was one contractor we worked with who would actually bankroll the construction and wait to get paid at the time the property was sold. That's how many deals were done in the beginning. Then ultimately, we went to a bank and got a line of credit. Even though the interest rate on that type of money was pretty high, double-digit, it was better than what we had, which was nothing. So not only did I have to come up with the program, I had to find out how to finance it, bankroll the program." Sam cautions CDCs not to "confuse nonprofit with not needing money. For those who desire to establish a community development corporation, they need to understand the business of business as well as the business of nonprofits."

Set It Up Right

Part of understanding the business of nonprofits is knowing how to set one up, something Sam has done for himself and others. He offers this advice to Christian CDCs. First, "distinguish the setup from the leadership." The setup is "fairly academic" involving creating articles of incorporation, bylaws, depending on the state, and getting state and federal tax-exempt status. "Many people might think they need to go to an attorney. Unless that attorney has experience in formation, they can't bring anything to the table. Unless that professional person, an attorney, accountant, or otherwise, knows various questions to ask and the right things to do, they might be providing a disservice to the end user. It's essential to get someone qualified, who knows precisely what they're doing."

Second, after the administrative setup is established, a church that wants to establish a successful CDC must find the right leadership to direct and run the CDC. Sam advises that the leader be "personable enough to deal with would-be funders." A good leader must also possess business acumen and "a certain level of confidence." While there is much the leader must "learn on the fly, there are certain inherent traits" that facilitate success. "So whether they're running a CDC or sailing the *Titanic*, there are certain leadership qualities—certainly Lula has them—that are fundamental to running an organization and managing expectations." Sam stresses the importance of managing expectations. "Not only must the leader manage the expectations of the board members that sit and serve with you but also, in the case of a faith-based CDC, the expectations of the church or a pastor or assistant pastor and leadership of that church. Some pastors believe, because they read the press, 'Oh, we set this up. We can get money. We can do all these housing deals. All this stuff can happen. Wow! This is good. Make it happen.' Whoa, let's slow down. We've got to crawl before we walk and walk before we run. And it might be a while before we can grow, right?"

Consider a Consultant

One important aspect of crawling before walking is knowing when it is both feasible and sustainable to hire staff. As an example, Sam considers the case of whether or not to hire a professional funder. "It could be a good thing if an organization has the wherewithal to bankroll it and the professional funder can bring value. So hypothetically, if the person is paid $50,000 a year and they're bringing in

$50,000 a year, there's no benefit. If they're paid $50,000 a year, and they can actually bring in something north of what their costs are to the organization, they bring value. I'm a big fan of adding value."

Alternatively, what WACDC did on occasion was bring on a professional funder as a consultant. The consultant was offered a very small up-front fee, and if the grant came through, they received an opportunity to work on the project. Sam adds, "But even in getting a piece of that, they were actually providing some of the deliverables associated with that particular grant. So often any grant has a project manager but aside from the project manager, there are some other activities and reporting requirements that need to take place that the consultant can do." This approach allows the consultant to realize "some cash and consideration" for their effort and faith in the organization. It also can be "less costly to the organization than hiring someone to come in full time where you're burning through cash, and it might very well take a year, two years, three years to actually realize any money." This form of fund development can be particularly beneficial to a faith-based CDC because "they often have an affinity or direct relationship to a church that is likely subsidizing the salaries of whoever might be on staff."

Employing human resource strategies that allow the CDC to both earn and save more money is wise. "Trust me," Sam says, "at West Angeles CDC, we're looking to make money. I will look to make money for the organization so we can be sustainable. This idea that at the end of the fiscal year there needs to be a net-zero—meaning you've raised a million, you spent a million—is erroneous. The tax code allows you to raise a million, or earn a million, and maybe you spend $700,000. The $300,000 is carryover. So as long as it goes toward those things articulated in the articles of incorporation, it's fine. And you just go on. So this notion of not-for-profit...no, we made a profit. It's just that whatever was made was carried over to programs for the next fiscal year. That's how it goes.

So, I think pastors, if in fact it's a pastor that's helping to lead this effort, and other board members need to understand the *business* of nonprofit community development corporations."

Sam notes that it is also important for people working in a nonprofit to get paid a fair wage. "There are some scandalous people out there. There are some people that have done quite well and they understand the system and they're still doing well for people in the community, but they're living a very prosperous life. Some people frown on that, and optics matter. I'm not saying that someone should take advantage of any situation, but do realize that if I have a 501(c)(3) nonprofit, the people working there can be paid. They can be paid market rate because they're doing, for lack of a better word, market-rate deals—real estate deals, business deals."

Render Unto Caesar

Sam explains that for-profit businesses pay taxes because, ultimately, their mission is to make money. Those taxes contribute to the public good by paying for things such as roads and schools. While a nonprofit can make money, it is not its mission to do so. Its mission is some public benefit, and this is why the government confers a tax-exempt status. Sam gives an example. "In terms of formation, you might have a C Corp that seeks to get recognized by the State Franchise Tax Board as being exempt from taxes because of its mission. If they are successful in doing that, then they have to apply to the IRS to be recognized as being exempt from federal taxes. If they are successful, then they are a tax-exempt nonprofit, in this case, public benefit 501(c)(3) organization. Typically, for those in the secular space and those in the space of community development and Christendom, if you will, they're likely seeking recognition by the federal government as a 501(c)(3). That's the one, I might add, that many funders like to see."

Sam describes the mission of the church, ultimately, as proselytizing. He expounds, "There's ministry—there are people preaching and teaching on Sundays and during midweek services within the walls. But people, also during those days, need food, housing, and a job." The impetus for West Angeles CDC is ministry beyond the four walls. Because of its separate nonprofit legal structure, the Christian CDC is able to seek monies from banks and other funders to do certain types of real estate deals, for example, that a church could not do without potentially losing its tax-exempt status. There are banks and other donors who simply "will not write a check to a church" because "they're not in the business of proselytizing."

The Christian CDC is a vehicle for the body of Christ to be, as Sam cites from the WACDC articles of incorporation, "a tangible expression of the Kingdom of God." While operating in accordance with the regulations dictated by "Caesar" (a biblical reference to the governing authorities), a properly structured Christian CDC can still render unto God what belongs to God—our love and service. Sam notes, "Jesus said that what you do for the least of these you do to me: feeding the poor, clothing the poor, building a house, helping out. There's a bed for somebody to lay their head on. There's food to eat. That's a tangible expression of that love you say you have for me. You love me—show me you love me."

> *For those who desire to establish a community development corporation, they need to understand the business of business as well as the business of nonprofits.*

PROGRAM DEVELOPMENT

Housing and Mediation Program Development

HOUSING DEPARTMENT NEW DEVELOPMENT: Specializes in the acquisition, rehabilitation, and construction of affordable family and senior rental housing throughout Southern California. Responsible for all feasibility, entitlement, financing, and construction issues related to the production of these apartments.

PROPERTY MANAGEMENT: Handles all on-site property management issues such as resident selection, on-going maintenance, rent collection, accounts payable and receivable, and resident relations.

SOCIAL SERVICES: Responsible for arranging all resident-related services such as computer training, after school programs, recreational activities, work training programs, etc. These programs are carried out by forging relationships with various outside service providers.

HOME BUYER EDUCATION: Department holds monthly 12-hour programs that teach community members the steps required to purchase and maintain homes. We also have an Individual Development Account (IDA) program which allows participants to deposit money into a local bank and have the funds matched when used for home purchasing purposes. Participants of both programs are provided with ongoing one-on-one counseling to assist them in obtaining their goal of homeownership.

EHOP PROGRAM: In this program, we work with the Enterprise Foundation by handling the project management aspects of rehabbing HUD-owned properties in designated areas. Once renovated, these homes are marketed to potential home buyers that qualify on an income-related basis for affordable housing.

EMPOWER Program – a Faith-Based Workforce Investment Act Project

The EMPOWER Program is a comprehensive service empowering men, women, and older youth who are striving to overcome critical barriers to gaining and maintaining employment.

EMPOWER services are offered in four phases:
- Phase One: Outreach, Intake, and Assessment of Skills and Career Goals
- Phase Two: Development of Life Skills, Computer, and Vocational Training
- Phase Three: Development of Interviewing and Resume Writing, and Job Search (Computer)
- Phase Four: Case Management, Job Placement, Retention

EMPOWER's participants include low-income individuals and ex-offenders, as well as persons in recovery for substance abuse. We service individuals who need to improve their job skills to become more job-ready in this age of technology. In addition, EMPOWER also assists high school drop-outs and those struggling with teenage pregnancy, poor work history, or other significant barriers to self-sufficiency as defined by the local Workforce Investment Board.

EMPOWER's Employment Advocates provide case management services for participants from assessment to job placement and retention. Follow-up services are continued up to one year.

EMPOWER coordinates services with other community resources, to meet immediate and long-term needs, ensuring that participants receive services that match their unique needs, skills, and interests.

EMPOWER accepts agency referrals as well as self-referrals. After intake and assessment, services will begin.

West Angeles Community Mediation Center

PEACEMAKER PROGRAM: The CMC reaches out to provide conflict resolution and prejudice reduction training to neighborhood schools. The PeaceMaker Program involves seven training components created to teach students, teachers, and parents the fundamental principles and skills to manage conflict and move beyond stereotypes to cultural understanding. The program provides schools with the capacity to be self-training and self-mediating within three years and provides nonviolence and diversity curricula as a standard part of students' education.

COMMUNITY MEDIATION SERVICES: The CMC is a full-service alternative dispute resolution center offering mediations, conciliations, and arbitration services to the community. The center provides trained neutral third parties to assist disputants in finding solutions that meet the needs of both parties. Fees for services are offered on a sliding scale that allows for most of our clientele to receive services at an affordable price.

COMMUNITY MEDIATOR CERTIFICATE TRAINING: The CMC provides several opportunities throughout the year for individuals to become certified as a volunteer community mediator. The certificate program consists of 30 hours of lecture, discussions, and role-plays. It prepares trainees to work on organizational, personal, community, and commercial problems. The training fulfills the requirements of the California Dispute Resolution Programs Act.

CERTIFIED MEDIATORS ADVANCED TRAINING WORKSHOPS: The CMC works in partnership with the Jenesse Center to bring education and intervention services to the community regarding the issue of domestic violence. In support of this initiative, the CMC has added domestic violence education curriculum to all other training programs. We also refer identified clients to the Jenesse Center for support services. Lastly, we are coordinating several performances of the "'The Yellow Dress," a one-woman show educating audience members in the realities and responses to dating violence.

MEDIATION AND CONFLICT RESOLUTION PUBLIC AWARENESS AND EDUCATION CAMPAIGN: Through staff and volunteers, we canvass the community with speaking engagements for community and social groups, churches, and conferences. We promote understanding of mediation, conflict resolution, and diversity training as viable peacemaking tools. In addition, the CMC uses the local media including radio, newspaper, and television to educate the community about mediation and the Center's activities.

Community Assistance Department

The mission of the West Angeles Community Assistance Department (CAD) is to provide emergency assistance and crisis intervention to individuals and families facing life's challenges through the provision of social services.

The philosophy of the CAD is "Compassion with Expectation." Our desire is not to become an enabler, further handicapping those in habitual need, but to provide a hand up out of their situation and not simply a handout.

We currently assist by providing:

- **Shelter Placement Referrals** – The CAD, though not in operation of any shelters, works along with those seeking emergency shelter by assisting in the location of shelters and providing appropriate shelter referrals, while attempting to help those in need navigate toward more permanent housing and self-sufficiency.
- **Referral Listing to Housing (Homes, Apartments, and Rooms)** – We provide listings to assist those seeking regular, subsidized (Section 8) and low-income housing. We work along with the West Angeles Housing Department to direct those seeking housing.
- **Emergency Food** – We provide emergency food to individuals and families once a month, unless extreme circumstances dictate otherwise. The emergency food is of a non-perishable (canned good items) nature.
- **Transportation Assistance Tokens** – Tokens are provided to assist individuals in transportation in these areas: shelter, medical, job search, non-medical emergencies, and case management services. Periodically, taxi vouchers are given to assist our senior population and those traveling to emergency shelter.
- **Transitional Living and Substance Abuse Programs** – We work to assist those with referrals in need of Transitional Living and Substance Abuse Programs. These programs are designed to provide a structured environment conducive to the total recovery of those with such addictions.

- **Job Referral & Placement Information** – Although the CAD is not set up as an employment agency, we provide information to assist individuals seeking permanent, temporary, and day labor. We refer individuals to various places such as One-Stops, Temporary Agencies, and agencies that assist in the development of skills that better qualify them for consistent work.
- **Hosting of Other Programs** – The CAD serves as a host site for many other community agencies to operate their programs through our services such as Energy Assistance Programs, Project Angel (DWP), Healthy SHARE, and "Feed the Children".
- **Referrals to Other Agencies** - Although we receive calls for many things that we do not handle, we make the heartfelt attempt to connect people with positive referrals.

SANDRA M. SPEED

Director of Housing

1996 – 2002

Sandra Speed was the Managing Director of Housing and Economic Development for the City of Pasadena when Grant Power, the Director of Economic Development at West Angeles CDC (WAC-DC), spoke with her about joining the CDC as Director of Housing. Not knowing exactly what that entailed, Sandra was hesitant.

Then she met with Lula Ballton!

Sandra describes the encounter. "Dr. Ballton has a very charismatic personality. So she pulls you into her vision. She was talking about her goals and plans and dreams for the CDC." Sandra was "mesmerized" and agreed to take the job. She left the City of Pasadena and her beautiful office with its "couch, TV, and everything" not realizing the "shift" she was about to make. Her new "office" at WACDC was called the Bridal Suite. Every time there was a wedding or anything pertaining to one, Sandra had to gather up all her belongings and find another place to work.

Find Funding

Locating a workspace was not the only thing Sandra was tasked with finding. As the Director of Housing, Sandra was responsible for finding ways to build housing for low- to moderate-income homebuyers and nice, affordable apartments for people in the community. West Angeles Church of God in Christ gave the CDC seed money to get the project started, but the development would be largely contingent upon Sandra finding sources of income for the project.

For her first project, West A Homes, Sandra had to negotiate for the purchase of the land. To the degree possible, Sandra sought businesses in the community, specifically African-American companies, for construction contractors, architects, and other roles required to complete the development. The project was funded with low-income housing tax credits, which, according to Sandra, are difficult to get because so many organizations compete for them. These tax credits paid for most of the construction. Sandra also developed a relationship with a woman in the Los Angeles Housing Department, with whom she says she is "still friends today," who helped the CDC understand how to secure funds to purchase the land.

Pray on the Job

With funding secured and property purchased, construction began. Sandra recalls, "It seemed like everything that could go wrong went wrong." Someone stole lumber from the construction site, and to Sandra, it appeared to be an inside job. "You had to have trucks and massive manpower to pick that [lumber] up and take it off." The security guard, who said he was working on the other side of the yard when it happened, claimed he did not hear any noise. But Sandra had her suspicions. At any rate the CDC had to purchase new lumber.

Then there was a disagreement between the architect and the project manager. Sandra told them both, "Every morning before we get started, we're going to pray. I don't care what your [faith] is. We just have to pray to my Jesus because this is going awry." Sandra describes one gentleman as "Asian and Buddhist" and the other as "Jewish." She recalls, "Once we started [praying], everything fell into place."

Make Connections in the Community

Across the street from West A Homes was Manual Arts High School. Before construction began, Sandra went to meet the principal. She told him about the development project, because, according to Sandra, it was the neighborly thing to do, and asked if Manual Arts had programs for the kids who would be living in West A Homes. The principal invited the West A kids to join the After School Program at the high school designed to assist youth in the community. He also told Sandra that if any of the West A kids attend Manual Arts High School, they could enroll in one of the specialized career tracks, such as finance, the school offered to help students get into college.

Sandra also connected with Joseph Loeb, a member of West Angeles Church, who owned a business that trained kids and adults in the community to work with computers and technology. Sandra told Joseph that she would like to have computers for the kids in West A Homes. Joseph connected her with a person from Sony, confident that they would "make a contribution" if Lula met with them and told them about the project. To Sandra's delight, Sony installed a computer lab, filled with brand new computers and the latest technology, into West A Homes.

Joseph also connected Sandra with Microsoft. "I talked to them and told them what we were doing," Sandra says. "[Microsoft] had a passion for giving to the community." They provided all the software for the computer lab. Sandra arranged with the principal for some of Manual Arts students to use the West A Homes computer lab. "Some of those [Manual Arts] kids who were very good with computers would help the [West A] little ones." Members from West Angeles Church also volunteered to tutor kids at West A Homes. Sandra credits God for these connections.

Sandra wanted to start a Bible study at West A Homes, but HUD rules and regulations prohibited the property developers from engaging in religious activities. A resident of the development, however, could lead a Bible study. So one of the residents volunteered and "put it together, and everyone came there and had Bible study." Sandra believes that offering volunteers meaningful work, not just "little tasks that you don't want to do," keeps them engaged and connected.

West A Homes, 44 units of beautiful, townhouse-style, affordable housing, won a Best Practices Award from the U.S. Department of Housing and Urban Development (HUD). "We won the [award]," Sandra says, "because not only was it a nice development, it was everything that we pulled together that made it a phenomenal project."

The grand opening of West A Homes was a proud moment for Sandra. Councilwoman Rita Walters' assistant, Jan Perry, was extremely impressed with the project, and she invited news reporters, who interviewed Sandra. There were photos of Lula Ballton and Sandra in hard hats. Sandra's teachers from the Minority Program in Real Estate, Finance, and Development at the University of Southern California came to join the celebration. There were "politicians…everybody…even my mom. It was amazing."

Help Those You Can

But not everyone who needed the affordable housing that West A Homes provided was ready to be helped. Sandra explains: "What happens sometimes is when you take people who were really poor and never really had anything nice, unless they do a renewing of their mind, they can't even conceive of something like what we put together." To illustrate her point, Sandra tells of a West A Homes resident who pulled a large garbage bin into her apartment. A few others were using drugs. Another woman was only allowed in because "her children were getting rat bites" at her former residence. Sandra recounts the story. "So we moved her in and her kids and then you go into her unit, it was like Hoarder Central. I told her, 'You're going to create the same environment there that you came away from where your kids will start getting bites.'"

HUD had strict regulations regarding government-funded developments, and the actions of these residents put the property at risk. Even though West A Homes was a WACDC development, HUD did not allow developers to control the application process. The West A Homes application process was handled by Barker Management. Sandra spoke with Peter at Barker Management, with whom she had become good friends. She told him, "We may have to evict some people or maybe just talk to them to see where their heads are at." Barker Management eventually evicted some residents to keep them from ruining the experience for everyone else. They were able to speak with others and encourage them to seek help.

Be Pragmatic

Sandra offers these practical tips to help Christian CDCs help those in their communities:

- **Be Strategic:** At any given time, there may be specific types of development that the government desires to fund. "When we did West A Homes," Sandra says, "multiple-family housing was a big deal," so it was easier to get that project funded. But she cautions, do not "chase the money." Follow your strategic plan. Sandra tells of a pastor friend who, distracted by funding opportunities, deviated from his strategic plan and pursued homeless housing development. The project was rife with problems because he was not prepared to handle all of the additional services, like drug, alcohol, and mental health programs, required to help the homeless.

- **Be Wise:** The faith-based community can sometimes be naïve, routinely assuming the best in people and taking them at their word. Some CDCs have paid thousands of dollars for land they never received. It is wise to vet potential project partners thoroughly, even if they are members of your church. Check their background. Talk with others who have worked with them. Make sure they have experience and an excellent track record in housing development.

- **Be Prepared:** Do your due diligence before attempting to pursue funding. For example, before you can apply for the low-income tax credits to do real estate development, you must prepare a proposal package, which can be expensive. You will need your pro forma budget, backing from the City, and the land acquisition virtually completed. These are but a few of the complexities which demonstrate the need for a qualified professional leading the project.

- **Be Political:** You need the support of the city councilperson where the land is located to complete a development project. Since low-income housing credits can be used for development but not for land purchases, the City will have to allocate a portion of its HUD resources to help purchase the land. You want to be confident that they are willing to do so.
- **Be Patient:** Understand that a real estate development project is "not going to happen overnight." It is a lengthy and complex process that requires many roles, such as a project manager, an architect, a construction contractor, a tax credit syndicator (an organization that purchases, manages, and leverages the tax credits), and a city or county representative to assist with advice and grant opportunities, among others. The benefit to the community, however, is well worth the effort.

Be a Role Model

The greatest benefit of housing development is that it develops people. Some of the West A kids who ended up going to Manual Arts High School came back to tutor other West A kids. One of those tutors is now a school principal. Another, a financier for Merrill Lynch, told Sandra that living in West A Homes made him want to pursue real estate development in order to give back to the community. Sandra's pride is evident as she relates his story. "He ended up on the financing side." He told Sandra, "'I always admired you.'"

Sandra reflects on the admiration she carries to this day for her own role model, Lula Ballton. "She was a great mentor. I was her problem child because I challenged her, but she was always right," Sandra says with deep reverence. "She was thoughtful and really committed to our mission." Sandra describes her perspective before coming to WACDC as "all about me trying to build my fortune, my brand, my name." Her priorities changed working at the CDC, "especially under Dr. Ballton because she's so selfless. She could have done anything or been anywhere. But she chose to work for the CDC. That's why Dr. Ballton is so blessed."

Sandra remembers telling her mother about her "dynamic boss" with a beautiful home, children in college, and a husband who was a banker. "I was telling my mom all the good things about Dr. Ballton, and she says, 'I didn't know your boss was a white woman.' I said, 'She's not.'" Sandra states the implication: "She connected all [Dr. Ballton's] success with being white."

Sandra makes her conclusion clear. It is imperative that we have those role models so we can "see ourselves doing those things." Sandra says that's why she helps those who seek her out. That's why she sits on a lot of boards, so she can help them manage their projects. She helps guide them to find funding so they can be successful. "You have to give back." Sandra believes that all churches can play at least some small part, even if they don't have a lot of money or assets, to help the community where their church resides. And they should.

ARIEL BAILEY FERNALD

Director, West Angeles Community Mediation Center
1996 – 2003

Ariel Bailey Fernald recalls her first lunch with Lula Ballton in 1994. For three hours, they discussed their dream to see not just individual transformation but systematic community transformation. "It was one of those moments where you think, I just found somebody that understands the very core of who I am and the purpose of what it is that I want to accomplish."

At the time, West Angeles had a K–8 Christian school. Although the school was, as Ariel describes, "outstanding academically," it shared the challenges of the community it was in. "The school reflected the entirety of that community"—students from broken homes with minimal resources to those from more affluent, two-parent families—all in one small school with a rigorous program. Ariel notes, "Any school with a strong academic program is going to have strong discipline."

Children were daily sent to the principal's office because of conflicts on campus, especially during recess. An example of a conflict requiring mediation would be one student's gossip about another avalanching into hurtful untruths. The target of the gossip becomes furious, thinking the other student spread malicious lies. The issue balloons into a classroom rift as other students take sides, refusing to work together, and into a lunch yard rift, with factions spoiling for a fight. Teachers cannot do their jobs as effectively in this environment. There were also some challenges with interactions between parents and teachers. When Lula heard about the mediation work Ariel was doing in different school districts, she invited her in as a consultant to help transform West Angeles Christian Academy.

Have the Right People in Place

Ariel is not merely a mediator but a conflict management professional, and there is an important distinction between the two. A mediator is someone who can work with two parties to help them explore the root of their conflict, identify the real issues of their conflict, and take them systematically through the process of mediation to resolve their conflict.

A conflict management professional has a broader scope. In addition to the role of a mediator, they must also be able to assess an organization, not just an individual conflict or situation. They must have the background that enables them to understand and assess cultures and be able from the assessment to identify the real conflict and its source, and then establish processes to resolve it. A

CDC starting a mediation center should consider hiring a conflict management professional to lead the program.

As Ariel designed the Scripture-based school mediation program she used in her consultancy before working with West Angeles Academy, she had the stunning realization that the school is the "institution of intersection" in the community. She explains, "Everybody's babies are in those schools and everybody has to get educated." The school is not just kids; it's families. Since the child is at the school, parents care about what happens at that school. Even individuals who do not have children are closely connected to families that do. This rippling effect expands into the broader community. "Churches are connected to that school because families from their churches go to that school. Social services serve families that go to that school. Businesses care about those schools because those schools have families who are their consumers. That's why they sponsor their football teams."

Following this revelatory line of reasoning, Ariel made the school the focal point of her program and connected not only with the kids but also parents, teachers, support organizations, and churches. She created overlapping conflict resolution programs to address the needs of each group. "It's like weaving," she says. The child changes best by seeing parents and teachers role modeling conflict resolution. "The expectation at home and at school is the same." The child hears the same powerful language of conflict resolution from parents, teachers, and organizational counselors.

Within two months of working with West Angeles Christian Academy, Ariel saw a change in the environment. "We performed an assessment and from it made recommendations for immediate changes as well as training. We first provided training for teachers and then for students to be leaders in Peacemaking. The principal reported back to me that the number of students waiting outside her office daily to be managed after recess because of playground conflicts went from three to five per recess down to three to five per week."

Ariel's mediation programs had a positive effect on teachers, students, and parents. "We were able to see a tremendous impact and a tremendous difference in the community. Then [Lula] said, 'Gosh, we need this.' And I said, 'We do.'" The County had been funding community mediation centers, and Lula and Ariel recognized that they had something special, something that worked. Lula and Ariel got "this crazy notion" that they could create a Christian community mediation center right in their own community specifically targeting the needs of the population they were working with. "There wasn't really a faith-based mediation center in the Los Angeles area," Ariel says. "So we said, 'We can meet a need for our community. We can expand to be a community mediation center. And we can incorporate faith if we do it ourselves.'" Thus the vision of the West Angeles Community Mediation Center was born, the goal of which was always to have a long-term impact—a greater, broader impact on the community.

Overcome Obstacles with Tenacity

After seeking God in prayer, Ariel began the daunting task of drafting a Los Angeles County proposal to secure a grant to establish the mediation center. Though she had written grant proposals for years, she had never encountered anything near the magnitude of the county proposal. But Ariel had an ace up her sleeve: WACDC's resident grant proposal writer, the "brilliant" Grant Power. Ariel often joked, "We have *grant power*; how can we lose?"

Still, the process was arduous. The proposal filled an entire three-ring binder, and the County required 12 copies. From the inception of the project, WACDC raced against the looming county deadline. Ariel recalls coming down to the absolute wire with only one notebook complete, though bleeding loose papers like a wounded animal. They threw the other copies of the proposal, in a nascent state of loose papers and empty binders, into a moving box and drove "like crazy people" through the maze of downtown Los Angeles to get to the county office before the noon deadline. Ariel recounts, "My poor intern said, 'We're not going to make it!' and I said, 'We're going to make it!'"

They pulled into the parking spot and continued stuffing papers into binders. But the clock was ticking. Everybody grabbed an armload, and they made it through the doors at 11:55. Ariel went to the clerk and handed her the only completed binder, still leaking papers. "I remember the woman looked at us—she was so sweet—she looked at us, and she said, 'Is this your proposal?'" Long pause. "'Okay,' the clerk said, 'I'll timestamp it for you.'" Ariel laughs at the memory. "She timestamped it 11:58. Then she said, 'Please go over to the desk or to the table over there and compile the rest of it. Just do that.'" So they spent an hour and a half in the county office putting their proposal in perfect order. But it was stamped at 11:58. "It was just the favor of God," Ariel declares. They were awarded one of the county contracts with its associated grant of $85,000 to start the community mediation center. "We had to prove to them that we were a viable vendor and that we knew what we were talking about. Even though we looked crazy, we had the right people in place."

With funding in place, Ariel joined the WACDC staff in 1996 as the director of the community mediation center and hired another one of the "right people," her "amazing and incredibly faithful assistant" Yvonne Hairston, who "knew nothing about mediation," but her superior organizational skills, attention to detail, willingness to learn, and thoughtful input made her "a tremendous asset" and the perfect complement to Ariel. Ariel stresses the importance of hiring staff with whom you can have "a partnership" for maximum efficacy.

Cultivate Qualities That Set You Apart

When asked what qualities set WACDC's proposed community mediation center apart, proving they were a viable vendor, Ariel replied that first, you need the person who has the passion and the professional credentials to lead. "Every organization rises and falls on leadership and, every leader rises and falls on their character and their communication," she explained citing a concept she learned from Christian leadership expert John Maxwell. Second, you need the program. You have to identify the specific mediation program your community needs. You must recognize that in *every* community, there is a need for conflict resolution, regardless of its location, socioeconomic standing, or ethnic makeup. Ariel explains that there is "not a community out there that has such an exemplary low divorce rate" or "criminal activity rate" that it cannot be lowered, or has schools so safe that they cannot be made safer. There is no place so perfect that it does not need a community mediation center, a "place of peace." Armed with that realization, you can identify the need in the particular community you endeavor to serve, the need you are uniquely qualified to meet.

The Christian community mediation center is "the place you go to help establish peace." Ariel expounds, "The Bible clearly tells us that blessed are the Peacemakers for they shall be called the children of God. And it's always stuck out to me that of all the things that God could have said that made someone His child, it was being a peacemaker." He who wins souls is wise, but it is the peacemaker who is His child. "[Jesus] was the great mediator between God and man. So when we really look like Him, we are mediating…And so the church should be the ones that are bringing mediation centers or conflict management centers into the community. That should be where people come to get mediation." But in order for that to happen, the church must mediate its own conflicts, as the Bible instructs.

Third, after the person and the program, you need the provision. "You have to be able to look into your community and find out where that provision is," Ariel says. One of the things Ariel learned as a conflict management professional was that most of the communities she desired to serve did not necessarily know that they had the funding to pay for mediation. Ariel had to become the expert at finding the funding. That journey for her began with a personal challenge issued by Lula Ballton.

Understand the Link Between Vision and Provision

As WACDC got bigger, Lula could no longer be the primary fundraiser. She challenged the directors to raise the resources for their departments. Ariel's budget had gone from $85,000 to $365,000. For Ariel, it was a trial by fire. One of her worst nightmares was being responsible for another person's livelihood, so she had always constructed her consultancy business with subcontractors. With the help of God and her husband, she found the strength not only to fund her vision but to help others fund theirs.

Ariel shares her insights. "God is faithful and will provide, but we also have to be realistic and know that we need to focus in on that [provision] from the beginning." The conflict management professional must first assess the need in the community and clearly define the vision of the mediation center to address that need. For example, in a city like Los Angeles, one issue in the community is conflict arising from cultural diversity. So perhaps a Christian mediation center could focus on cultivating cultural harmony amidst cultural diversity. That's the vision.

For the provision to fund the vision, look not only for conflict resolution resources available at the city, county, and state levels but also for, in the case of our example, cultural diversity dollars. Look in what Ariel describes as "multiple pools of resources" for funding that complements the specific type of conflict resolution your mediation center will provide. "Define your program and its priorities from that need and then your provision will match the need."

Beyond government funding, seeking grants through foundations is "absolutely key," Ariel advises. Find organizations that "share your vision or some part of your vision" and write effective grant proposals, but don't stop there; develop a relationship with the foundations. Regarding WACDC's funding success, Ariel asserts, "It was not just writing good proposals; it was developing relationships because the relationships sustain the organization. [The foundations] became invested in us and every year wanted to see us continue." One of WACDC's relationships was with the venerable Ahmanson Foundation, which strives to enhance the quality of life and cultural legacy of the Los Angeles community by supporting nonprofit organizations that demonstrate sound fiscal management, efficient operation, and program integrity. A "very generous and consistent supporter," the Foundation also connected WACDC to other grant foundations which supported similar projects. Having a credible qualified professional running a program not only helps to ensure the excellence and effectiveness of the program but also goes a long way in helping to secure the funding.

An often overlooked source of funding, according to Ariel, is fee-for-service profit. A nonprofit can "go out and make money" as long as the extra money goes back into the organization. For those clients who can afford to pay something, offer sliding-scale fees, providing the service at a drastic discount. "Someone who normally would pay a $125 fee coming to our center might only be paying $50. They're still being blessed because we are a community organization, but we are also receiving funds." Another example is charging a sliding-scale fee to a school. "It's so important that a school has buy-in and that they have skin in the game. If you are given anything, people take it for granted. So I would say to them, 'You need to come up with $1,500, minimum. I'm going to work with you all year. I'm going to do trainings. I'm going to work with your staff, your kids, your parents. I'm going to be mediating for you. You're going to come up with $1,500, and you're going to commit to me X number of hours.'"

Further, Ariel advises to "think outside" the funding sources she has already delineated. "You have to think about who your client is." Most West Angeles Community Mediation Center clients came through referrals from church members, WACDC Emergency Service clients who needed assistance mediating with businesses or individuals to help resolve their circumstances, or members of school communities. "So again, I will go to a school and they would say, 'We need you so bad, but we have no money.' And I'd say, 'Are you a Title 13 school?' I would ask if they were under certain titles in education. And then if they said yes, I'd say, 'You have money. You can use that money for this." It is imperative that you be the expert in finding funding. "I had to know better than some of my clients where their money was." Then the decision was theirs whether or not to use that money for mediation, but Ariel was firm. "I'm not going to use all my time and my money that we've raised to work with you. When you're not willing to put in that 10 percent, I'm not putting in the 90."

To those schools that don't have Title I money, those that think they have nothing, Ariel says, "You have parents. You have a community. You have kids. You can do a fundraiser." Such schools can do a big fundraiser at a single event, or they can sell candy over six months and make the same amount of money. In either case, they can feel good about themselves as individuals and as a community because they are contributing to the transformation. They have learned how to fish.

Becoming the provision expert requires education. Ariel took grant proposal writing classes on Saturdays in her free time. "You're investing in the future," she says, "and making the vision happen." Some volunteer organizations, such as OneOC (*www.oneoc.org*), formerly Volunteer Center of Orange County where Ariel took her classes, the largest and most comprehensive of the 250 volunteer centers nationwide, not only offer volunteer recruitment but also teach nonprofits how to write grant proposals, establish budgets, host fundraisers, and even how to choose an appropriate fundraiser for your level of organization. While this full-service volunteer center focuses on serving Orange County, California, you can search the Internet for volunteer centers near you. Ariel also educated herself about the types of funding specific to her conflict resolution areas of specialty, such as the Title 13 funding for schools. Ariel was driven by her passion to see vision provisioned in the communities she served, which is why she strongly advises that passion and professionalism be paired in the person directing the mediation center.

Put Character Before Success

In addition to passion and professionalism, the Christian mediation center director must have character. One of the things that surprised Ariel most in her career was encountering conflict management professionals who achieved success in mediation that was incongruent with their character. They learned mediation formulas and applied them well. They simply played a role. Since the organization, however, rises and falls on leadership, the director cannot be merely an actor playing a role.

The mediation center is volunteer-driven, with a web of mediations working in the community. "You cannot have internal conflict and externally be helping people," Ariel asserts. She has interacted with conflict resolution professionals who had a reputation for helping others but were themselves terrible at dealing with people in person. "I was in the home of a conflict resolution professional and watched her flip out on her husband and almost break the sliding glass door in the back of her house." Ariel describes another scene with the same individual. "I watched her as she was speaking horribly in handling a conflict with the assistant of a Superintendent's office that we were working with."

How do you avoid hiring such an individual? Ariel suggests that you ask them casual questions about their personal and peer relationships during an interview or lunch. Why did they leave their last job? How would they describe their boss? What are things about their boss that they liked or didn't like or would want to change? How did they feel about their coworkers at their last job? Listen carefully as they talk. You will learn a lot about that person—how they handle people, how they see people, how they personally interact. If a conflict resolution professional cannot use the skill set in their own life, it will ultimately be a problem for the mediation center. It will come out. It will be a problem for your reputation.

Seek Transformation

Placing a high premium on character, find a leader you can trust and trust them. Ariel recalls, "Lula prayerfully and carefully found the leaders over the different areas. And once she found that leader, she instilled in us a sense of confidence. We knew that she had confidence in us. I felt encouraged; I felt respected for the professional that I was. And that is really important for someone to flourish." Build on the character of your leader to create a mediation center whose heartbeat is transformation.

Ariel credits Bishop Blake of West Angeles Church with the "sandwich approach" to community transformation. She explains the concept. "You have to work with the people at the top and you've got to work with the people at the bottom. It has to be simultaneous. That's where you really see the community transformation."

Transformation is grassroots, and it is legislative. Both are necessary. Ariel has heard Bishop Blake say, "I have to do my job. I'm preaching to the people down here, and I'm establishing programs that are going to help at the very bottom. And I'm also having lunch and meeting with and ministering to people at the very top."

Ariel's face is lit with passion. "I want to see the world transform...I believe mediation centers have transformative power." Your CDC may not look like West Angeles CDC. It may not have emergency services, mediation, housing, economic development, but God can show your church how your CDC can be transformative in your community." So ask God, how can I serve my community? "We need to know how to step out of the church doors and impact the community with intention."

> *Build on the character of your leader to create a mediation center whose heartbeat is transformation.*

THE STEPS TO
FOLLOW

This section describes the suggested steps to take to start your Christian Community Development Corporation. While the steps follow a logical progression, they need not be accomplished in any rigid order. For example, you may opt to Set Up the Legal Entity before you Select Board Members. Each step has a checklist containing a set of action items to accomplish. Like the steps themselves, there are cases where it may suit your situation to alter the order of the steps. We suggest you read through this entire guide to build a mental framework of the activities involved in starting a Christian CDC and then refer back to each section as you actively work toward accomplishing the mission to which you have been called.

STEP 1: **Define the Identity of Your CDC**

STEP 2: **Select Board Members**

STEP 3: **Set Up the Legal Entity**

STEP 4: **Create a Strategic Plan**

STEP 5: **Develop Programs**

STEP 6: **Develop Funding**

STEP 7: **Hire and Manage Staff**

Step 1: Define the Identity of Your CDC

Your identity as a Christian Community Development Corporation will be defined by your unique, God-imprinted response to the community you desire to serve. Defining the unique identity of your CDC will set the tone for how you impact the community. Do it prayerfully. The checklist below identifies the suggested tasks to accomplish to complete this step. These items need not be performed in any rigid order. For example, you may already know like-minded individuals who would be excellent candidates for a steering committee. You might, therefore, opt to form the steering committee earlier in the process to assist with writing the vision and mission statements.

ACTION ITEMS

✓ **Engage the Community: Define the Need**
✓ **Define Geographic Boundaries**
✓ **Explore Existing Organizations**
✓ **Write Your Vision and Mission**
✓ **Form a Steering Committee**

✓ Engage the Community: Define the Need

Before you begin building a community for Christ, you must have an answer to the fundamental question: "What does my community want?" The answer or answers to this question will be the first step towards creating a Christian CDC. Jesus did not force Himself on others but asked them, "What would you have me do? Do you want to be made whole?" The Savior then met them at their point of need. Similarly, we should minister first to what people feel are their areas of need. Doing so is a matter of respect.

Community engagement is a vital component of developing a successful CDC. *Coming Up with the Money: Five Principles for Launching a Successful Community Development Initiative*, a guide produced by the Community Development Department of the Federal Reserve Bank of St. Louis, states, "The importance of engaging the community is grounded in the belief that the public has a right to participate and to articulate what their needs are." Community engagement not only helps to get a truer assessment of the needs in the community but also involves residents in problem-solving and decision-making. Generally, it is better to involve community residents early in the process to get higher levels of buy-in.

Research the community you hope to serve. Interview people in that community. Go to the places where the people congregate (e.g., churches, festivals, parks, etc.). Attend community events. Conduct community forums. Start networking. Address issues that are important to the people actually living in a community. Do what you can to discover these issues and then prioritize them according to urgency. And stay connected. Community engagement is an ongoing process occurring throughout the existence of your CDC.

Want to learn more? NeighborWorks America (*http://neighbor-works.org*), an intermediary organization which builds the skills, supplements the funding, and amplifies the reach of grassroots organizations so they can leverage additional resources to achieve their missions, offers training in community engagement.

SOURCE: *https://www.stlouisfed.org/-/media/files/pdfs/community-development/comingupwithmoney/comingupwmoney2016.pdf?la=en*

AS EASY AS ABCD

One empowering application of the principles of community engagement is Asset-Based Community Development (ABCD). A strategy documented by John McKnight and John Kretzmann in their 1993 guidebook, *Building Communities from the Inside Out*, ABCD assesses a community's assets and capacities—including resident skills and local organization and business strengths—and leverages them to help develop the community. West Angeles CDC has used this approach since the inception of the CDC, long before they became aware of the codified version. Lula believes that the community already has inherent wealth—in the people. It is the job of the Christian CDC to unearth that wealth and put it on display, first so the community can behold their true selves, as in a mirror, and then those outside the community will be enlightened as well. ABCD is a glass-half-full approach which supports the existing strengths in a community to drive and sustain change.

You can learn more about ABCD from the Asset-Based Community Development Institute founded by McKnight and Kretzmann at DePaul University (*https://resources. depaul.edu/abcd-institute/Pages/default.aspx*).

✓ Define Geographic Boundaries

As you engage and connect with the community, the character or flavor that makes it a uniquely cohesive community will become clearer to you. In other words, you will begin to see where the community you wish to serve begins and ends. This knowledge will be helpful as you decide how broad your outreach will be. You must determine the geographical scope of your outreach. You should be able to identify street names, freeways, or geographical features such as a river, to specify the community you serve. For example, West Angeles CDC's target area is South Los Angeles, roughly bound by Adams Boulevard to the north, Vermont Boulevard to the east, La Brea Avenue to the west, and Manchester Boulevard to the south.

Formalizing the geographic boundaries of the community you serve assists your marketing efforts and communication with government officials and investors, allowing you to identify your community with specificity as an important area worthy of their attention. You must also know the community boundaries for grant proposals.

You can find helpful ideas on defining neighborhood boundaries at *https://www.useful-community-development.org/neighborhood-boundaries.html.*

✓ Explore Existing Organizations

After you discover what needs should be met, explore how existing organizations may already be addressing those needs. Ask yourself, "Is a whole new organization justified?" It may be the case that the duplication of the efforts of other groups is not warranted. Even if these existing organizations are less than optimal in meeting the identified needs, it may be possible to reform these groups rather than creating a whole new organization from scratch. Starting and sustaining a CDC will take a great deal of work and time. Make sure that you are ready to take on the challenge of starting one for the long haul.

✓ Write Your Vision and Mission

Answering the question, What does your community want? sets the stage to create a vision statement for your organization. A carefully crafted vision statement is at the heart of every successful organization. This statement clearly and concisely communicates your CDC's overall goals and can serve as a tool for strategic decision-making across the organization.

You may choose to write your vision and mission statements now or wait until after you have formed a steering committee to garner more input. In either case, it will most likely be an iterative process as you are starting your CDC. It may be helpful to go through this exercise on your own to clarify your own vision and mission to help you better articulate it to others in the community. Once the steering committee is formed, as a team you will review, and may opt to revise, the statements. Once the board of directors is selected, the vision and mission statements can be reviewed and formalized.

A vision statement can be as simple as a single sentence or can span a short paragraph. Regardless of the individual details and nuances, all effective vision statements define the core ideals that give an organization shape and direction.

Before you begin, it is important to understand the distinction between a vision statement and a mission statement, as many confuse the two. Mission statements are designed to explain why the organization exists to both members of the CDC and the external community. It describes what the organization is doing in the present. Vision statements, on the other hand, describe where your organization is going, what it will achieve in the future. Vision statements are designed to inspire and direct employees, rather than clients. A mission statement answers the question, "Why does my business exist?" while a vision statement answers the question, "Where do I see my business going?"

The vision of West Angeles CDC is inspired by this description of Zion in Zechariah 8 (CEV). As you read the passage, let the vision of the Beloved Community inspire you to see your own community, not just as it is, but as what your Christian CDC can help it to become:

The LORD All-Powerful said to me:

[2] I love Zion so much that her enemies make me angry. [3] I will return to Jerusalem and live there on Mount Zion. Then Jerusalem will be known as my faithful city, and Zion will be known as my holy mountain.

[4] Very old people with walking sticks will once again sit around in Jerusalem, [5] while boys and girls play in the streets. [6] This may seem impossible for my people who are left, but it isn't impossible for me, the LORD All-Powerful. [7] I will save those who were taken to lands in the east and the west, [8] and I will bring them to live in Jerusalem. They will be my people, and I will be their God, faithful to bring about justice.

The vision of West Angeles CDC is to see the community it serves transform into the Zion it is called to be. For examples and tips about how to write a vision statement, see: *https://www.businessnewsdaily.com/3882-vision-statement.html*

After you have the vision of where your CDC is going, a mission statement will emerge from answering the following three questions:

- What is your calling?
- What is your ministry's purpose?
- What is its identity?

The answers to these questions comprise the mission of your ministry.

By way of example, let us take a look at the West Angeles CDC mission statement: *To increase social and economic justice, demonstrate compassion, and alleviate poverty as tangible expressions of the kingdom of God through the vehicle of community development.*

Notice how specific and actionable the mission statement is as contrasted with the vision statement. The mission of West Angeles CDC is not conducting worship services or observing the ordinances of the church, but rather to increase social and economic justice for God's glory through the vehicle of community development. Similarly, your CDC will have a specific mission to fulfill. Below is the full West Angeles CDC mission statement as an example:

CALLING:

God has called West Angeles Community Development Corporation (West Angeles CDC) to promote justice and peace, demonstrate compassion, and eradicate poverty as tangible expressions of the Kingdom of God through the vehicle of community development. West Angeles CDC subscribes to community development as a liberating process aimed at *Economic Empowerment, Social Justice, and Community Transformation.*

IDENTITY:

- West Angeles CDC operates within the greater ministry and vision of West Angeles Church of God in Christ supporting the linkage between church and community.
- West Angeles CDC represents an effort by believers in Jesus Christ to reach out in witness and ministry based on the conviction that the Gospel of Jesus Christ is relevant to and able to significantly impact the community in which they live and serve.

West Angeles CDC is a part of a broad movement of Christian churches seeking to promote social change through Christian Community Development.

PURPOSE:

Economic Empowerment

- To develop and foster programs and enterprises which provide lasting employment opportunity
- To actively engage community leaders, residents, business leaders, and others in planning, implementing, and evaluating development projects
- To develop and rehabilitate affordable, low-and mixed-income housing in and around the Crenshaw area
- To serve as a base for technical assistance and community development strategizing in Los Angeles

Social Justice

- To foster conditions of economic and social justice by local participation, mobilization of community resources, and raising people's awareness of their ability to shape their own future
- To promote literacy and creative educational initiatives among adults
- To advocate for and administer English as a Second Language (ESL) curricula in meeting the educational needs of a burgeoning Latino population

Community Transformation

- To facilitate greater understanding and reconciliation through *Community Dispute Resolution*
- To demonstrate God's transforming power working in whole communities as well as individuals' lives

For another example, here are the vision and mission statements of Habitat for Humanity:

VISION: A world where everyone has a decent place to live.

MISSION: Seeking to put God's love into action, **Habitat for Humanity** brings people together to build homes, communities, and hope.

CORE PRINCIPLES: Demonstrate the love of Jesus Christ.

✓ Form a Steering Committee

At some point during your initial thinking about the needs of the community and the community engagement process, gather together people with the same or similar vision as yours in order to talk both informally and formally about these needs. Invite those who are most interested and committed to join a small steering committee. If you have already drafted your vision and mission statements, you will want to get input from the steering committee and make revisions as necessary. Members of the steering committee may not continue with the CDC after it is formed, but they will engage in the hard work of forming it.

Do not be discouraged if members of the steering committee do not stay for the long haul. If their interest is flagging or other activities draw them away, graciously release them and keep moving forward as you seek a replacement if necessary. You may consider qualified members of the steering committee who show the greatest commitment to the CDC to be candidates for placement on the initial board of directors.

Step 2: Select Board Members

Before you can select a quality board of directors, you need a thorough understanding of what boards do. Nonprofit board seats are a profound responsibility. Take great care in developing your board of directors. Your board will determine the direction of your CDC.

ACTION ITEMS

✓ **Understand Board Member Responsibilities**
✓ **Select Founding Board Members**
✓ **Identify Continuing Board Members as Required**
✓ **Train Board Members**

Before discussing board member responsibilities, you should understand some basic nuts and bolts required for an operationally healthy CDC. First, know that a CDC is a *business* that should make a profit. (That profit is used for the *public benefit*.) Any good business needs systems that work and also needs to be productive. Second, a healthy CDC will need appropriate and adequate legal counsel. Third, the CDC will need to be financially viable and accountable. I recommend that you hire an accountant with expertise in not-for-profit corporations so that your organization can keep accurate books. Now, applied to this basic framework, our discussion of board member responsibilities will have the proper context.

Fundraising and ensuring adequate funding is one of the primary responsibilities of a nonprofit board of directors. Although they are not primarily in the business of generating revenues, bottom lines are just as important to nonprofits as they are to for-profits. The board of a Christian CDC, in particular, has a higher ethical imperative than just ensuring the health of the organization's bottom line. The board must advance the God-given mission of the CDC and serve as representatives of the community.

The board is the governing authority of a CDC and looks to the executive director and staff to implement its policies. It is incumbent upon the full board to set policy, not individual members however strongly they may feel about an issue. Understanding this principle helps the board to operate not fractiously but rather as a cohesive unit.

✓ Understand Board Member Responsibilities

You will need a clear articulation of board member responsibilities. Board Source identifies ten basic responsibilities of nonprofit boards:

1. **Determine mission and purpose**. It is the board's responsibility to create and review a statement of mission and purpose that articulates the organization's goals, means, and primary constituents served.

2. **Select the chief executive.** Boards must reach consensus on the chief executive's responsibilities and undertake a careful search to find the most qualified individual for the position.

3. **Support and evaluate the chief executive.** The board should ensure that the chief executive has the moral and professional support he or she needs to further the goals of the organization.

4. **Ensure effective planning.** Boards must actively participate in an overall planning process and assist in implementing and monitoring the plan's goals.

5. **Monitor and strengthen programs and services.** One of the board's foremost responsibilities is to determine which programs are consistent with the organization's mission and monitor their effectiveness.

6. **Ensure adequate financial resources.** One of the board's most vital responsibilities is to secure adequate resources for the organization to fulfill its mission.

7. **Protect assets and provide proper financial oversight.** The board must assist in developing the annual budget and ensuring that proper financial controls are in place.

8. **Build a competent board.** All boards have a responsibility to articulate prerequisites for candidates, orient new members, and periodically and comprehensively evaluate their own performance.

9. **Ensure legal and ethical integrity.** The board is ultimately responsible for adherence to legal standard and ethical norms.

10. **Enhance the organization's public standing.** The board should clearly articulate the organization's mission, accomplishments, and goals to the public and garner support from the community.

FIDUCIARY RESPONSIBILITIES OF BOARD MEMBERS

One of the main responsibilities of board members is to maintain financial accountability of their organization. Board members act as trustees of the organization's assets and must exercise due diligence to oversee that the organization is well managed and that its financial situation remains sound. Fiduciary duty requires board members to stay objective, unselfish, responsible, honest, trustworthy, and efficient. Board members, as stewards of public trust, must always act for the good of the organization, rather than for the benefit of themselves. They need to exercise reasonable care in all decision making, without placing the organization under unnecessary risk.

Not every board member can be a financial wizard. Every board member, however, needs to be a financial inquisitor. It is essential to understand basic terminology, be able to read financial statements and judge their soundness, and have the capacity to recognize warning signs that might indicate a change in the overall health of the organization. If a board member does not understand something, he or she must be willing to find out the answer.

Specific questions board members should ask:

- Is our financial plan consistent with our strategic plan?
- Is our cash flow projected to be adequate?
- Do we have sufficient reserves?
- Are any specific expense areas rising faster than their sources of income?
- Are we regularly comparing our financial activity with what we have budgeted?
- Are our expenses appropriate?
- Do we have the appropriate checks and balances to prevent errors, fraud, and abuse?
- Are we meeting guidelines and requirements set by our funders?

Determine what types of programs your organization can provide and who will make these programs possible. Various program-related questions that must be answered include:

- How do you identify what is needed?
- How do you start these programs?

- How do you maintain your programs?
- How do you retrain staff?
- How do you attract resources?

BoardSource.org is a helpful resource that offers training for board members.

✓ Select Founding Board Members

Initial board members are usually invited by the incorporators, the person(s) who formed the legal entity, to join the board. But who do you choose? The members of the steering committee who show the greatest interest in the CDC effort may be candidates for placement on the initial board of directors. Most nonprofit boards have between three and 25 directors.

Following are some recommended selection criteria:

- As a Christian CDC, the majority of your founding board members should be committed Christians. This will help to ensure that you develop and cultivate a pervasive Christian culture in your CDC.
- Board members must have character and integrity.
- They must believe strongly in the mission. If they do not bring this critical quality to the table, their value will be reduced, regardless of the other skills they possess.
- They must exhibit business or organizational competency. They need not be business leaders, but they should understand sound business principles.
- They should be strategic thinkers.
- They should be willing and able to give of their time *and* money to see the CDC's mission accomplished.

Candidates will possess these qualities at varying levels. While some criteria, such as character and integrity, are non-negotiable,

the key is to seek a board where these qualities are present and balanced as a whole, rather than necessarily in a specific individual.
SOURCE: *www.501c3.org/nonprofit-board-members-choose-wisely/*

✓ Identify Continuing Board Members as Required

While your start-up focus will be on selecting founding board members, have a future eye toward seeking and identifying candidates for continuing board members.

What is the difference between founding and continuing board members?

A continuing board member may be an initial board member, but that is not necessarily the case. Someone, for example, may be able to contribute to the founding of an organization, but may not have the time or the energy for a long-term commitment to that organization. When searching for continuing board members, the utmost care and research should be done to find the very best candidates. It is possible for someone who is committed to an organization (as should be the case for initial board members), to not have the appropriate skill set or available time to help run that organization.

Qualifications for successive board members are the same as those for initial members. As opportunities occur to fill vacated spots and to add new ones, remember the quest for balance. Continuing board members should be chosen judiciously. They should thoroughly understand the organization's vision and mission. They also should have a positive history of service and success in the community. They need good communication skills and must be willing to work together with others in order to make decisions that, although tough, will ultimately benefit the organization.

The key consideration for selecting continuing board members, however, is that the selection process is done according to your CDC's bylaws. Bylaws must always be rigidly followed, or someone may issue a legal challenge which could put the CDC in jeopardy of a violation of state corporate law and IRS 501(c)(3) requirements. Consider seeking the help of someone with experience to aid you in drafting your bylaws. It is worth noting here that there may be attorneys, accountants, or other professionals you are considering inviting to your board. Only select such candidates if they meet all of your other selection criteria, not because you think you can get free professional advice. Legal and professional help should be independent in most cases to avoid potential conflicts of interest. SOURCE: *www.501c3.org/nonprofit-board-members-choose-wisely/*

✓ Train Board Members

You have already based the selection of your board members on their commitment, experience, and expertise, but there is always room for growth. Exceptional boards embrace continuous learning, not only for those in their organization but also in themselves.

Seek out training opportunities for your board members. One place to start is BoardSource (*BoardSource.org*), a recognized leader in nonprofit board leadership, which supports, trains, and educates nonprofit leaders from across the country and throughout the world.

Step 3: Set Up the Legal Entity

It is vital that you set up your CDC properly as a legal entity. It is wise to enlist the aid of an attorney or consultant experienced in nonprofit formation. Though incorporating your new organization is listed here after selecting your board, you could opt to incorporate before selecting the board. The articles of incorporation are usually signed by an "incorporator," which can be just one person. The articles can also be signed by the initial board of directors if they are named in the articles. If the founding directors are not specified in the articles, the incorporator can and should appoint the board through a written action. An advantage of selecting a board before you incorporate is the benefit of their collective wisdom and experience to help your draft bylaws and generally assist with the complexities of the incorporation process.

ACTION ITEMS

✓ **Understand the Legal Terms**
✓ **Understand the Faith-Based CDC Distinction**
✓ **Incorporate as a Community Development Corporation**

✓ Understand the Legal Terms

The terms *nonprofit, tax-exempt,* and *501(c)(3)* are often used interchangeably, but legally, they mean three distinct things.

Nonprofit, also called a Nonprofit Organization (NPO), is an entity, usually a corporation, not organized for the purpose of making a profit.

Tax-exempt is a tax status resulting from a nonprofit organization being recognized by the Internal Revenue Service (IRS) as being organized for any purpose allowable under tax codes 501(c)(3) through 501(c)(27).

501(c)(3) is a tax exemption in the United States Internal Revenue Code given by the IRS only to organizations that provide religious, educational, and charitable service. A nonprofit organization that has been recognized by the IRS as being tax-exempt because of its public-benefit programs under code 501(c)(3) is often referred to as a "501(c)(3)" or a "501(c)(3) nonprofit." There are different types of 501(c)s, 501(c)(3) being the most common, and the one donors most like to see because of the tax write off it affords them. Some examples of 501(c)(3)s are: American Red Cross, Salvation Army, Goodwill Industries, and Habitat for Humanity.

Benefits of 501(c)(3)
A few of the benefits of being a 501(c)(3) nonprofit are:
- Receive donations that are tax-deductible to the donor
- Exempt from paying federal and/or state taxes (though you must in some cases still file a return)
- Qualify for grants and other public or private funding available only to 501(c)(3) organizations
- Leverage the credibility of IRS recognition

✓ Understand the Faith-Based CDC Distinction
Religious organizations may opt to form faith-based CDCs for some of the following reasons:
- to protect the organization and its assets
- to be eligible for government and foundation funding that might not be available to a church
- to build an organization to separate the Church from activities funded by the government

When forming a faith-based CDC, the relationship between the church and the new Christian CDC must be clearly defined and properly structured:

- Both organizations should have separate bank accounts, accounting records, stationery, and board of directors.
- If the church and CDC share staff, the arrangement and the responsibilities of each staff member should be clearly delineated.
- The church may transfer assets, such as money, computers, or use of space, to the CDC if the church board approves the donation.

✓ Incorporate as a Community Development Corporation

Before you can apply to become recognized as a 501(c)(3) nonprofit organization, you must first incorporate as a nonprofit organization (NPO).

Incorporating a faith-based CDC is involved and time-consuming. We strongly recommend having experienced professionals involved—such as attorneys, board members with nonprofit incorporation experience, and experienced consultants—to protect your interests, make sure you have structured and filed everything correctly, and ensure that all legal requirements are met. You may be able to secure an attorney willing to incorporate your nonprofit organization pro bono, but again, experience is key. Incorporation is handled at the state level and is dependent upon the religious corporate laws and the nonprofit laws of the individual states.

Here are the basic steps to incorporate a nonprofit organization:

1. **Choose a business name** – Make sure to check the state-by-state information on the various laws that apply to naming a nonprofit in your state.

2. **Appoint a Board of Directors** – These are the founding board members. These directors should understand their

duties and responsibilities to act with reasonable care and in the best interests of the organization while providing direction and oversight over the organization's activities, finances, officers, and legal compliance. Board requirements can be different in each state, so be sure to check the laws in your state. Under California law, for example, a nonprofit board may have only one director, but the IRS is not likely to grant 501(c)(3) tax-exempt status to a nonprofit with only one director. Most nonprofits have between three and 25 directors. These are considerations that an experienced professional can help you navigate.

3. **Draft Bylaws** – Draft your bylaws with guidance from your board of directors. These are the operating rules for your nonprofit, and you will have to adhere to them.

4. **File your incorporation paperwork** – You must next file formal paperwork, or articles of incorporation, and pay a filing fee to your state, typically less than $200. The articles of incorporation outline basic principles of your CDC, such as your CDC's name, duration of its planned existence, exempt purposes, specific purposes, membership, directors, prohibitions, dissolution conditions, registering agent and office, incorporator's name, and indemnification clause. Your articles of incorporation must contain the correct verbiage for a tax-exempt 501(c)(3) corporation according to IRS rules. Note that if you do not have the correct statements in regard to your nonprofit intent and your willingness to abide by 501(c)(3) tax code's rules, then you probably will not receive a letter of recognition of tax-exempt status from the IRS and you will have to un-incorporate your flawed corporation and start the process again. This is why enlisting the aid of an experienced professional is so important. You can look up your state office through the National

Association of State Charity Officials (NASCO) for your state-specific instructions to file your articles of incorporation. Note that someone will have to pay the State fees for incorporating in cash or out of their personal account, as you will not have any of these tax identification numbers before you incorporate and you cannot have a bank account for your corporation until you incorporate.

5. **Hold board meeting to take initial board actions** – The board will adopt bylaws, elect officers, approve establishing a bank account, approve filing for tax-exempt status, approve reimbursement of start-up fees (if applicable), approve compensation of the executive director (and others as applicable), and approve other necessary actions.

6. **Obtain an employer identification number (EIN)** – An officer or authorized agent can obtain an EIN online. You will need an EIN to open a corporate bank account.

7. **Apply for federal 501(c)(3) tax-exempt status** – Complete Form 1023 for exempt status under Internal Revenue Code (IRC) Section 501(c)(3). The filing fee is currently $850 for most organizations. The IRS may typically take three to four months or longer to process a Form 1023 application for exempt status, longer if there are errors or missing information on the form.

8. **Obtain necessary licenses and permits** – Ensure that your nonprofit has all the licenses and permits required to comply with federal, state, and local laws.

9. **Apply for state tax-exempt status** – After you receive a 501(c)(3) federal determination letter from the IRS regarding your federal tax-exempt status, file for state

tax-exempt status. Check with your state for specific instructions.

While churches are not required to file annual tax returns, separately incorporated faith-based CDCs must do so. To understand and comply with this and other legal matters, be advised that federal and state regulations are extremely complex and you should, therefore, seek proper legal counsel before proceeding.

SOURCES:

- *www.usa.gov/start-nonprofit*
- *www.501c3.org/frequently-asked-questions/does-nonprofit-501c3-and-tax-exempt-all-mean-the-same-thing/*
- *www.hud.gov/sites/documents/CFBNPPRACGDE2014.PDF*

Step 4: Create a Strategic Plan

Now that you have committed to starting a community development corporation, it is time to create a strategic plan. A road map for your CDC, the strategic plan charts your course, outlining your goals and the strategies to achieve them.

ACTION ITEMS

✓ **Understand the Value of a Strategic Plan**
✓ **Create a Strategic Plan for Your CDC**
✓ **Edit and Finalize the Strategic Plan**

✓ Understand the Value of a Strategic Plan

Strategic planning is a process that helps focus on aligning the unique gifts and resources that God has given your organization to take advantage of your opportunities. Simply put, a strategic plan is a working document that describes how your organization executes your chosen strategy.

A strategic plan is a management tool that serves the purpose of helping an organization do a better job, and it improves organizations because a plan focuses the energy, resources, and time of everyone in the organization in the same direction. Strategic planning does not have to be mysterious, complicated, or time-consuming. In fact, it should be quick, simple, and easily executed. Additionally, strategic planning is not just something you cross off your list of "to-dos"—you must create a culture of strategic thinking, so your strategic planning does not become merely an annual retreat activity but, instead, a part of daily decision making.

A good strategic plan achieves the following:

- Reflects the values of the organization
- Clearly defines what is most important for achieving success
- Assists everyone in daily decision making
- Gets everyone on the same page, focused and pulling in the same direction
- Creates a culture of strategic thinking in daily decision making

A strategic planning process identifies strategies that will enable the CDC to achieve its mission. At its most basic, a strategic plan crystalizes:

VISION—where are we headed in the next one to five years, and
ORGANIZATION-WIDE STRATEGY—how we will get there

Active participants in the strategic planning process are more likely to commit to measurable goals, approve priorities for implementation, and revisit the CDC's strategies regularly. Tying strategic initiatives and discussion to the agenda for board meetings will help the board remain engaged in the strategic planning process.

✓ Create a Strategic Plan for Your CDC

Drafting a strategic plan transforms ideas into concrete action items—a critical step to achieving forward momentum for your CDC. A clear strategic plan will also assist your fundraising efforts and build community support.

The Basic Components of a Strategic Plan

A strategic plan should minimally include the following components:

- a review of the CDC's vision, mission, and values
- an outline of strategic goals, objectives, and activities

- an assessment of current resources
- a strategic analysis

Each section is generally several paragraphs to several pages in length.

Review Vision, Mission, and Values
The first section of the strategic plan should be a strategic review of your CDC's vision, mission, and values as they set the stage for all that follows. Since your CDC will be mission-driven, it is important to put careful and prayerful thought into reviewing and internalizing the mission that will guide your organization for years to come.

Specify Strategic Goals, Objectives, and Activities
This section of your strategic plan involves breaking down your broad mission into concrete, specific goals, which will facilitate the creation of concrete plans. For example, if your mission is to create better economic opportunities for single mothers in your community, you might devise the following specific goals: offer training in job skills, provide resume and mock job interview clinics, publicize job opportunities, mentor mothers in career development, teach entrepreneurial skills, and provide or subsidize childcare.

You can then get more specific and devise objectives (concrete, measurable sub-goals) with deadlines. Continuing the example above, let's focus on the goal of teaching entrepreneurial skills. One objective might be to develop a curriculum by a specified date. It is difficult to discern if a broad mission has been achieved, but a set of specific objectives can easily be measured.

Clearly defining planned activities and programs that align with your objectives will advance your mission. Not only will this portion of your strategic plan help you manage your operations, it will also help you engage the community and attract funding.

Assess Your Resources

This section of your strategic plan should contain a detailed assessment of all of your resources currently available to the CDC. Include human resources, money, skills, expertise, and other assets. This is not a fundraising plan but rather a realistic accounting of what you already possess.

Identify Strategies

With the planning in the other sections complete, you are ready to devise strategic planning, practical ideas and plans to creatively use your resources to achieve your goals. A common approach to facilitate strategic thinking is called a "SWOT" analysis to assess Strengths, Weaknesses, Opportunities, and Threats that are strategically important to your Christian CDC. SWOT is a filtering tool to assess where you are now. Strengths and weaknesses are positive and negative elements inside the organization; opportunities and threats are positive and negative elements outside the organization.

Examples of SWOT Elements
- Strengths are positive assets inside your CDC. For example, a well-connected, charismatic leader, a large pool of dedicated volunteers, or valuable copyrighted curriculum.
- Weaknesses are negative aspects inside your organization. For example, a limited pool of volunteers or the recent retirement of a popular leader.
- Opportunities are positive elements outside your organization. For example, a strong relationship with a funding partner, the availability of a new grant, or a high demand for one of your programs.
- Threats are negative elements outside your organization. For example, a new city ordinance that restricts your program offering or the loss of a major grant.

An important part of SWOT analysis is creatively leveraging your strengths and opportunities to help mitigate weaknesses and threats.

✓ Edit and Finalize the Strategic Plan

After you complete your strategic plan, let it rest for a couple of days and then, with fresh eyes, look for opportunities to improve it. Set a deadline so the revision process does not go beyond its usefulness to a point of diminishing returns. Once you have completed your final edit, you may opt to package your strategic plan professionally for external use—to present to potential donors, for example—and less formally for internal use.

Want to Learn More?

For more practical information on creating your strategic plan, as well as information on getting a nonprofit off the ground, see *Starting & Running A Nonprofit: A Practical Guide*, by Peri H. Pakroo, J.D. (Nolo).

- *www.councilofnonprofits.org/tools-resources/strategic-planning-nonprofits#sthash.EKnl70lK.dpuf*
- *Every Nonprofit's Tax Guide*
- *How to Form a Nonprofit Corporation*
- *Starting & Building a Nonprofit*
- *Nonprofit Fundraising Registration*

Step 5: Develop Programs

Now that you have taken action on setting up the administrative component of your CDC, it is time to develop your own unique programs that will demonstrate the love of Christ in your community. Do not be deterred by the rigorous nature of program planning. Any CDC seeking grant funding must go through this process. The time and energy spent will be well-rewarded by effective and efficient programs.

ACTION ITEMS

✓ **Understand Keys to Successful Program Planning**
✓ **Understand Guidelines to Manage Program Planning**
✓ **Develop Program Framework**
✓ **Design Program**
✓ **Plan Program Implementation**

✓ Understand Keys to Successful Program Planning

Carter McNamara, an expert in nonprofit program development, provides an excellent framework for understanding and executing program development in his book *Field Guide to Nonprofit Program Design, Marketing and Evaluation.* This section provides a brief summary of his method. For details, see *https://managementhelp.org/ programmanagement/business-programs.htm#anchor4294895830* and *https://managementhelp.org/programmanagement/nonprofit-programs. htm.* For an in-depth treatment, refer to his book.

Six Cornerstones for Solid Program Planning

McNamara offers six "cornerstones" for strong yet flexible program planning:

- Programs Should Tie to the Organization's Mission
- Program Planning Should Tie in with Strategic Planning
- Involve the Board
- Conduct Program Planning as a Team
- Program Planning Should Involve Potential Clients as Much as Possible
- Don't Worry About Developing a Perfect Program Plan

Programs Should Tie to the Organization's Mission

Starting from the mission, during strategic planning, the organization's leaders must define the major goals that, when reached, accomplish the mission.

Program Planning Should Tie in With Strategic Planning

Each goal that the board identified during strategic planning typically becomes a program. The strategies to reach a specific goal become the framework, or roadmap, of the new program.

Involve the Board

Since it is the responsibility of the board to chart the direction for the organization, they should work closely with the executive director to guide the initial direction of new programs.

Conduct Program Planning as a Team

The program planning team should consist of designated board members, the executive director, program managers, and major clients.

Program Planning Should Involve Potential Clients as Much as Possible

The input of key clients, as the end users of the program, is invaluable in the initial and final stages of the program planning process.

Don't Worry About Developing a Perfect Program Plan
Even if you bring in consultants, trust that the unique makeup of your CDC, anointed to do God's work, makes you the ultimate experts on your own program planning. Trust your instincts.

✓ Understand Guidelines to Manage Program Planning

Eight Guidelines to Keep Program Planning on Track
McNamara offers eight guidelines to not only keep your program planning from gridlock but also help ensure that your program is effective and efficient.

- Focus on Outcomes
- Examine Your Intended Outcomes – Conduct Some Basic Marketing
- Coordinate the New Program with Other Current Programs
- Explore if Client Services Can Be Delivered More Effectively via Collaboration
- Plan Key Indicators of Program Success
- Include Short-Range Focus in a Long-Range Plan
- Learn by "Testing the Waters"
- Plan Program Reviews

Focus on Outcomes
Outcomes are the benefits your clients receive from your program. A useful service well-delivered is the mission and North Star of the CDC.

Examine Your Intended Outcomes – Conduct Some Basic Marketing
Used here, marketing indicates community engagement to conduct marketing research, ensuring there is a need in the community for your program before you develop it. Marketing also helps you determine how your clients want the services delivered and how much

they are willing to pay—yes, pay. A sustainable CDC must seek opportunities to generate revenue so it is not excessively reliant on external funding. Use this research opportunity to coordinate your new program with compatible existing programs to provide an ecosystem of service to your clients.

Coordinate the New Program with Other Current Programs

The new program is but a part of an overall system. Pay close attention to current programs and to how the new one will coordinate with others in the organization. Ask these questions: What inputs are needed from other managers? What ongoing feedback is needed among members of the new program and other programs? How can the new program benefit existing programs?

Explore if Client Services Can Be Delivered More Effectively via Collaboration

Successful collaboration is the synergy of two or more organizations working in tandem to create something more than the sum of their parts. Collaboration can also reduce cost through economies of scale and shared resources. Further, more funders are requiring collaboration planning as part of their application process.

Plan Key Indicators of Program Success

Key indicators are concrete ways to measure the success of your program. Identify the key indicators that represent a successful program. For example, number of clients served, homes saved, taxes prepared, teens mentored, money made, client satisfaction as measured by surveys, etc.

Include Short-Range Focus in a Long-Range Plan

In a three-year program plan, for example, the way you focus on and plan year one will be different from year three. Presumably, you may be able to project one year out than you can three years out. Therefore, view your plans as guidelines rather than rigid rules, being strategically adaptable when a strong enough reason presents itself.

Learn by "Testing the Waters"

Be open to planning a six-month or one-year pilot, a mini-program reflecting key elements of the full program. Gather reviews and assessments from the pilot program to inform planning for the full program. In some cases, funders are more willing to fund a pilot to test the waters.

Plan Program Reviews

The executive director, a board member, the head of the new program, and one or two other program directors should participate in periodic reviews. The aim of such reviews is to assess the efficacy of the new program using key indicators, ascertain if the program has deviated from the program plan without good cause, address significant concerns, and evaluate lessons learned from the implementation to date.

✓ Develop Program Framework

The components of McNamara's program framework are:
- Program Outcomes
- Program Goals
- Program Strategies
- Program Objectives

Program Outcomes

As noted before, program outcomes are the benefits clients receive from your program. For example:
- Program Outcome 1 – Single parents earn entrepreneurship certification.
- Program Outcome 2 – Within three months after getting certified, participants start small businesses.

Program Goals
Program Goals should be specific, realistic, and measurable.

- Program Goal 1 – Support 500 single parents to obtain entrepreneurship certification.

Program Strategies
Program strategies are the methods your CDC will use to reach each goal.

- Program Strategy 1.1 – Conduct entrepreneurship certification training programs for single parents.
- Program Strategy 1.2 – Offer subsidized childcare to enrollees.
- Program Strategy 1.3 – Provide free transportation to enrollees.
- Program Strategy 2.1 – Offer small business microloans to certified participants.
- Program Strategy 2.2 – Provide mentorship from business leaders in the community.

Program Objectives
Program objectives are smaller, specific, measurable milestones for each goal.

- Program Objective 1.3.1 – Provide six vans to transport eight riders each per day to and from training.
- Program Objective 1.3.2 – Provide 50 bus tokens to attendees per day

✓ Design Program
The next step is to design each service your program offers by writing responses to each of the prompts below. A service is a closely related set of activities with a specific benefit to your client. For example:

- Service for Outcome 1 – Entrepreneurship training services
- Service for Outcome 1 – Childcare services
- Service for Outcome 1 – Transportation services

Write a basic description for each of your services.
Your description should include the nature of the service, the specific group of clients to be served, outcomes, other benefits, pricing, location, quality, atmosphere, what prospective clients should do if they are interested, etc. Describe it all in terms of benefits to your clients, not to you.

What groups of clients will you serve?
Identifying your target market will help your program to be more effective and inform you in advance where to target your marketing efforts. Think not only of your primary market but also secondary markets where you should focus promotions. Include a profile of each customer type.

- Target Market 1: Single parents in South Los Angeles
- Target Market 2: Churches in South Los Angeles
- Target Market 3: Business associations in South Los Angeles

What needs will your services meet for each target market?
Specify the major needs being met, describing them as benefits to the clients and secondary markets.

- Needs Met for Target Market 1 – Entrepreneurial skills and a second source or new primary source of income
- Needs Met for Target Market 2 – Place to refer single-parent church members who are struggling financially
- Needs Met for Target Market 3 – Additional program to offer members and potential members

Who will be your competitors?
If other nonprofits in your community offer the same or similar service, how will yours differ or be better? Research their offering to help improve your own.

Who will be your collaborators?
Explore and consider other organizations with whom you could collaborate to the mutual advantage of all parties.

What should you charge?
Funders will not support programs indefinitely. Charging your clients, below-market, for example, gives them skin in the game and provides your CDC with revenues to maintain the program.

What laws and regulations must you follow?
Contact local and state agencies to determine laws and regulations that affect your services.

What will you call your service?
Carefully select an appealing name that you can brand and promote. Choose well; it may be around for a long time.

Do you need copyrights, trademarks, or patents?
Protect any intellectual property you create from this process for the benefits it may bring your CDC and prevent others from using your name and perhaps tarnishing your brand.

✓ Plan Program Implementation

After you have designed your program, you must plan how you will promote, deliver, measure, and fund your program.

Plan Program Promotions
Program promotions include planning advertising and public relations. You can also include planning for sales and customer service.

Plan Service Delivery Methods

Service delivery involves planning methods to produce and distribute your services.

Plan Methods to Measure Program Success

This planning step involves building in key indicators of success, conducting the pilot program, and having periodic reviews to assess ongoing program performance.

Plan Resources and Budget

Carefully plan the resources required to execute your program, including personnel costs, training, space, equipment, materials, etc., and create a program budget.

Step 6: Develop Funding

"Fund development is the essential partner of philanthropy. Fund development makes philanthropy possible by bringing together a particular cause and the prospects and donors who are willing to invest in the cause. The goal is to acquire donors of time and money who stay with the charity." – Simone Joyaux, *Basic Principles of Fund Development*

ACTION ITEMS

✓ **Understand the Basic Principles of Fund Development**
✓ **Identify Potential Funders**
✓ **Solicit Funds**

✓ Understand the Basic Principles of Fund Development

Developing and securing long-term donors is all about developing and securing long-term relationships. Over 70 percent of public-benefit charitable funding comes from individuals rather than corporations and foundations. Even when the funding source is a foundation or corporation, it is still individuals within those organizations making funding decisions. Individuals thrive in flourishing relationships. While professional fundraisers and consultants are available to assist you, as well as fundraising training programs, understanding that good relationships undergird and perpetuate your funding endeavors will help you be successful at achieving your funding goals.

Basic Principles of Fund Development

Robert Payton, the former head of the Center on Philanthropy at Indiana University and Purdue University, defines philanthropy as voluntary action for the common good[1]. Effective fund development is simply connecting would-be donors with causes they care about. Your funding development goal for your CDC is to acquire donors (of both money and time) who will remain with you. This goal is accomplished through building relationships that foster mutual loyalty and value.

So what does this mean in practical terms?

Understand the three classifications for a potential individual or organizational funder:

1. **The Predisposed**: One whose interests and actions suggest a *possible inclination* toward your cause.

2. **The Prospect**: One who has demonstrated an interest in your cause or organization, perhaps by joining your mailing list or buying your service.

3. **The Donor**: One who has given a gift of time or money or service to your organization.

Keep these classifications in mind as you apply these tips to your fundraising methodology:

- Nurture a **culture of philanthropy** in your organization. It's the right attitude that matters as much as anything. Culture refers to the personality or attitude of your organization. A culture of philanthropy means that everyone accepts and celebrates the beauty of philanthropy and donors, no matter the type or size of the gift.
- Build a **donor-centered**[2] organization. Focus on the donor or prospective donor: "It's not what your organization is

selling; it's what I'm buying that counts. I'm interested in my interests, my motivations, and my aspirations. Match those and then I'll give to you. Otherwise, leave me alone!"

- Don't universalize your own passion. Not everyone is interested in your cause, no matter how convincing you are. Do not try to convince them! That's offensive. Instead, find those who share your passion.

- Giving is an **emotional act**, not a financial transaction. Your organization is the means by which donors live out their own interests and aspirations. Neuroscience and psychological research document that all human decisions are triggered emotions[3]. Then rationale steps in. Research from the direct mail industry says that people give in response to one or more of seven emotions: greed, guilt, anger, fear, flattery, exclusivity, and salvation. People move from one emotion—e.g., anger—to hope, by using your agency as the means to make the change. Tom Ahern refers to this partnering of emotions as "twin sets."

- Engage **volunteers**, including board members and others. Make sure your staff effectively enable volunteers to participate in this meaningful work of identifying, cultivating, and soliciting.

- **Don't trespass** on personal and professional relationships. Instead, use connections to identify those who might be predisposed to your cause. If you cannot qualify them as prospects (and it's their choice!), then leave them alone. Nurture relationships between prospects and your organization, getting them ready to be asked and asked again.

- Effective fund development is like **permission marketing**[4]; people opt in or opt out. "Permission marketing is the privilege (not the right) of delivering anticipated, personal and relevant messages to people who actually want to get them...treating people with respect is the best way to earn their attention. Permission doesn't have to be formal but it has to be obvious." (from Seth Godin's book and blog)

- More **visibility** does not produce more contributions. Everyone focuses on his or her own interests: Your agency can be more and more visible—"but if I'm not interested, I'm not paying attention. And I sure won't send money."
  - It's okay if someone doesn't know who your agency is or what it does. Tell them, if they're interested. That's identifying the predisposed.
  - Do not solicit someone unless you know for sure that the person knows about your agency.
  - Where do you need to be visible? Among your current donors, because you want to build their loyalty. Absence does not make the heart grow fonder—it's out of sight and out of mind! Nurture these donor relationships.
- *You* have to **give first**. (*You* means each board member, the CEO and development officers, and fundraising volunteers.) Why? Because you cannot represent an agency or cause without demonstrating your own financial and volunteer investment. Build an **individual giving program**. Each year, individuals give the largest portion of philanthropic gifts in North America, and individuals are more loyal donors than foundations or corporations.
- Fund development is a **process and a profession**. The profession is founded on ethical principles and standards[5], based on a well-researched body of knowledge[6], and protects the public through voluntary certification of professionals. Personal opinion—without the body of knowledge—doesn't and shouldn't count for much.
- Most **fund development problems** are actually not fund development problems. Most problems relate to other

areas of operation. Fix the real problem. (See www.simone-joyaux.com and click on Learning Center / Free Download Library / Fund development / *Choosing your road*.)

■ A **balanced funding mix** of solicitation strategies and donor sources ensures stability and credibility. Whenever possible, the best way to solicit a gift is through face-to-face solicitation.

✓ Identify Potential Funders

Initial Funding

The best sources of initial funding for your Christian CDC will be individuals and organizations with whom you already have a relationship. Look to the church associated with your CDC and to board members and their connections. You can also host fundraisers commensurate with your available resources. Many funding options will not be available to you until your CDC has 501(c)(3) tax-exempt status and a track record of successful initiatives. Below are a few other funding options to help you begin your exploration.

Grants

Grants are the financial lifeblood of any nonprofit. There are four primary sources of philanthropic giving: individuals, corporations, foundations, and bequests—with more than 70 percent coming from individuals.

Grant proposal writing is a skill, and you should consider seeking an experienced grant writer as a consultant or staff member to assist you. Grant writing and fundraising training courses, like those offered at *OneOC.org*, are also available and would help to bring a valuable skill set to others in your CDC.

For more information on grants and philanthropy, see:

■ CANDID *https://candid.org/find-funding*
■ GIVING USA *https://givingusa.org/*

Federal Government Grants

There are traditionally two types of federal grants available: the first type is awarded directly to the recipient from a branch of the federal government, and the second type is federal money given to states, cities, and communities for them to distribute to charities and social service providers. Though government funding has been in decline, the second type of grant generally has more money available of the two because there is less competition at local levels.

You can start your search at:

- *https://www.grants.gov/*
- *https://www.hud.gov/grants*

State and Local Grants

State and local grants may be easier to procure. Here are two starting points to begin your search:

- The annual "State Administrative Officials Classified by Function" issued by the Council on State Government.
- Your state's agency directory, normally available from your local library or from the office of your Secretary of State.

Suggested resources:

- *Getting Funded – A Complete Guide to Proposal Writing* by Susan Howlett
- *The Only Grant-Writing Book You'll Ever Need* by Ellen Karsh and Arlen Sue Fox
- *Winning Grants Step by Step: The Complete Workbook for Planning, Developing and Writing Successful Proposals* by Tori O'Neal-McElrath

✓ Solicit Funds

Why do most people give? Because they are asked. It's really that simple. We have not because we ask not. But ask only those who are interested. Ask the right prospect for the right amount at the right time for the right project in the right way with the right solicitor. Once you have done your research and identified your list of potential funders, following the principles of funding development, have the courage to ask. Talk to that individual, plan that fundraising event, write that grant proposal. Not every solicitation will garner a *yes*, but if you are resilient and adaptable, enough will.

ENDNOTES

1   Phrase coined by Robert L. Payton, first professor of philanthropics in the U.S. and former head of the Center on Philanthropy at Indiana University / Purdue University in Indianapolis.

2   See Donor Centric Pledge in *Keep Your Donors* and at *www.simonejoyaux.com.* Click on Learning Center / Free Download Library / Fund Development / Relationship Building.

3   See the research of Dr. Antoine Bechara and Dr. Antonio Damasio, described in Tom Ahern's books on donor communications. *www.aherncomm.com.* By the way, psychologist W. Gerrod Parrott identifies many more than seven emotions. Read all about emotions in *Keep Your Donors: The Guide to Better Communications and Stronger Relationships,* by Joyaux and Ahern.

4   Term introduced by Seth Godin in his 1999 book *Permission Marketing.* Godin contrasts permission marketing to interruption marketing, the traditional advertising/marketing approach. You know, the billboards and glitzy ads—and sending me a newsletter that I didn't ask for.
    So you identify the predisposed—those you suspect might have interests similar to your cause/organization—and introduce yourself (personally is usually best, e.g., through a cultivation gathering or one-on-one). Then, if the person (or corporation or foundation) expresses interest, that gives you permission.

Godin observes: "Rather than simply interrupting a television show with a commercial or barging into the consumer's life with an unaccounted phone call or letter [or in fundraising, the newsletter or a solicitation], tomorrow's marketer [and top-notch fundraiser] will first try to gain the consumer's consent to participate in the selling process."

5   See the *Donor Bill of Rights* and the *AFP Code of Ethical Principles and Standards of Professional Practice* at *www.afpnet.org.* Or visit *www.simonejoyaux.com/learning-center/education-certification/*

6   Visit CFRE International (*www.cfre.org*), the baseline certification for fundraisers worldwide. Click on the Test Content Outline, which describes the required knowledge for a fundraiser with five years of experience.

SOURCES:

- From *Keep Your Donors: The Guide to Better Communications and Stronger Relationships.*

- See Donor Centric Pledge in *Keep Your Donors* and at *www.simonejoyaux.com.* Click on Learning Center / Free Download Library / Fund Development / Relationship Building.

- Read all about emotions in *Keep Your Donors: The Guide to Better Communications and Stronger Relationships,* by Joyaux and Ahern.

- Basic Principles of Fund Development - Simone Joyaux *www.simonejoyaux.com/downloads/ BasicPrinciplesOfFundDevelopment.pdf*

Step 7: Hire and Manage Staff

A good Human Resources department is indispensable to the running of an effective organization. A company's staff could be its most valuable asset if properly managed or its most costly liability if not. Read books and seek professional assistance to learn the basics of successful human resource management. Provide a positive and fair environment for your employees.

ACTION ITEMS

✓ **Assess Organization Needs**
✓ **Recruit, Screen, and Select**
✓ **Orient Staff and Volunteers to the Organization**

Like any for-profit organization, staffing decisions are among the most critical that a CDC will make. Your programs can only be as excellent as the people developing and executing them. In addition, a nonprofit has the task of managing volunteers. Your CDC must address the following six personnel issues, as outlined in the Small Business Administration publication *Human Resources Management:*

- Assessing personnel needs
- Recruiting personnel
- Screening personnel
- Selecting and hiring personnel
- Orienting new employees to the organization
- Deciding compensation issues

Peter Drucker, in *Managing the Non-Profit Organization,* asserts,

"An effective non-profit manager *must* try to get more out of the people he or she has. The yield from the human resource really determines the organization's performance. And that's decided by the basic people decisions: whom we hire and whom we fire; where we place people, and whom we promote. The quality of these human decisions largely determines whether the organization is being run seriously, whether its mission, its values, and its objectives are real and meaningful to people rather than just public relations and rhetoric."

✓ Assess Organization Needs

Before you can effectively staff your CDC you need to have an accurate assessment of your organization's needs, both present and future. You must factor in the internal needs of the CDC, such as planned initiatives and budget, and the external influences of your environment, such as legislative changes and layoffs, all within the context of your mission.

Gary Roberts, Carlotta Roberts, and Gary Seldon note in *Human Resources Management* the following business principles regarding effectively managing personnel:

- Fill positions with people who are willing and able to take on the job.
- Provide accurate and realistic job and skill specifications for each position to help ensure that it will be filled by someone capable of handling the responsibilities associated with that position.
- Provide written job descriptions, an essential tool for communicating job expectations.
- Choose employees because they are the best available candidates, rather than on the basis of friendship or expediency, as they are far more likely to have a positive impact on the organization.

- Couple performance appraisal with specific job
  expectations to help boost performance and morale.

✓ Recruit, Screen, and Select

Recruiting

Letting the community know that you exist is the most important
action you can take to recruit both staff and volunteers. Nonprofits
use two basic methods to do this: local media (newspapers, news-
letters, radio advertising, billboards, etc.) and other community
organizations (municipal governments, churches, civic groups, other nonprofit organizations, etc.). As a Christian CDC, you have
the added opportunity of recruiting staff and volunteers from the
church associated with your CDC, who are likely to share the mission and thus be more willing to get involved.

Screening and Selection

Conducting effective interviews is essential to staffing, and it is as
important for volunteers as for paid staff. The process must be systematic. Use the following tips during staffing, screening, and selection:

- Realize that all personnel—employees and volunteers—
  regardless of position or hours worked have an impact on
  the group's performance. A poorly-performing, unethical,
  or unpleasant person can have an enormously negative
  impact on your CDC.
- Use thorough job applications.
- Make sure screenings cover skills, knowledge, and attitudes.
- Determine if the applicant is interested in the organization
  for the right reasons (professional development, interest
  in your mission, concern for the community) rather than
  reasons that do not advance your mission (loneliness,
  corporate burnout, just seeking a paycheck).

- Evaluate applicants based on criteria established in the job specifications.
- Have reasonable expectations of volunteers.
- Accommodate both strengths and weaknesses because everyone has both. Seek the combinations that work best for CDC.

✓ Orient Staff and Volunteers to the Organization

It is vital to have a training program for both new employees and new volunteers. The program should not only provide training for their position but also training to facilitate their integration into the team and the work of the CDC. Following these steps will help your CDC to have a thriving, cohesive team. Treat your employees and volunteers with concern and respect. Look to their interests, and they will look to yours.

SOURCES:

- Center for Faith-Based and Neighborhood Partnerships Practical Guide. U.S. Department of Housing and Urban Development, 2014 *https://www.hud.gov/sites/documents/ CFBNPPRACGDE2014.PDF*

SUSTAINABILITY

Now that you have the tools to start your CDC, here are strategies to keep it growing strong:

- Develop Systems for Board Evaluation and Rotation
- Standardize Systems for Increased Control
- Refine Methodology
- Develop and Maintain Personnel
- Improve Cost Recovery
- Expand Donor Base
- Refine Methodology
- Establish a Niche
- Join Associations for Learning and Policy Impact

SUMMARY

I have always been interested in how words transcend both the natural and the spiritual. Words speak things into being. As an attorney, people's lives can depend on the words I use. I have also always been engaged in civil rights. I use language instead of violence to change hearts and minds. As the cofounder and executive director of West Angeles CDC, I used words to create a vision. How do we help people see themselves as the Lord sees them?

The most important thing as the leader, particularly the founding leader, is to be a business-oriented person who creates the scenario for the organization—the vision. My posture has always been as the leader that you don't need to know everything. You need to know and understand the field. You need to have a vision, a point of view, and a direction. The next best action you can take is to hire experts. I was very particular about whom I hired because I wanted to avoid what often happens to nonprofits and government agencies—people are hired who have no experience, no understanding of the field, and then they practice on the poor people.

My approach to achieving my vision for Christian community development was to find people who were experts. That way, rather than trying to teach them their craft, I taught them the vision of the CDC, gave them parameters, and asked them to "vision." I asked my staff of experts, "How far can *you* go in your arena of expertise? How much can we bring to God's people through the skills and gifts and talents God has given you?" I openly displayed my respect for their knowledge and position. That is how you can create a team that all pulls together toward a vision you each own.

Follow your vision onto the streets of the community to which you belong, the community you are called to serve. Being a part of the community is one of the most important things you can do to develop relationships in the community because the relationships already exist for you to build on. It is important to let the community know, first and foremost, "I am not coming to do something for you or to you. I'm coming to understand what you want and to just see—if I were to bring these experts that I have around me together with what you want—what we can all accomplish together. Show them the beauty of their community, a people and a place worthy of love and attention and respect and investment. Show them the amazing assets their community contains and how you can work together to leverage them. Show them the beauty of who they are inside, and let that knowledge transform the geography.

Turn Challenges into Opportunities

Teach and empower your community to recognize its value and to be self-sustaining. Our communities don't know how to be self-sustaining. I didn't understand how to do it either. So I educated myself—taking classes, going to city government, going to developers, talking to people, listening, listening, and more listening, until I understood. As the leader of a Christian CDC, you can do that too. First, you have to see it that way. You have to see the value and potential in the people and the community before you can make anyone else see it. Look closely, with God's eyes, and you will see the value and the beauty.

But it will not be easy. One of the biggest challenges I faced was ensuring that the CDC had the resources to execute our vision. One strategy I used was to keep West Angeles CDC from being the typical 501(c)(3), moving from grant to grant. Some donors give because they can get the tax deduction to increase their bottom line. That's a business decision for them. The business decision for the CDC needs to be making ourselves so valuable and viable that we are "hired" to get a community development project done because we do it so well.

My approach with city government, for example, was to underscore the fact that it was their commitment to the taxpayer to use our tax dollars to deliver urban development, such as a playground for kids. I asked, "What are your plans for my urban area? Oh, you don't have any particular plans? You just have a sum of money you are going to dispense in my area? Well, because it's your job to dispense, *contract* with me. I am excellent. Examine my track record or do a pilot program to see what we do. But instead of coming back every year begging you to give me some money to keep it going, I want to contract with you. You tell me what results you need. I'll tell you what I can do. And as business partners, you contract with me to provide excellent housing. You contract with me to lower violence in your public school." You make a business relationship out of what you do so that the people you're doing it with and for understand that neither you nor your clients are objects of charity. You're getting paid by the government to create programs so children's lives are changed. They can do it directly, which is neither their inclination nor expertise, or they can pay you to do it. It is not charity. Your mindset—your perspective and approach—can turn very real challenges into very real opportunities.

You will find surprises as well as challenges. One thing that surprised me was once institutions—foundations, the government, all of them—understood what we were doing and saw the benefit to themselves, how quickly they got on board. An unpleasant surprise, on the other hand, was how long it takes to make change. If you want to build housing, for example, it may take you over a year to do all the pre-development: get all the paperwork done, all of the political tasks done, and all of the social and civic tasks done. But once all of it is done, it only takes a year to build it.

Seek God's Uniqueness

Plan to stay for the long haul and recognize that you can't do it alone. Ask the Lord to send you the specific people you need. Lay your requests before Him. That is how I "found" my amazing staff. I didn't find them at all. God sent them to me. Also, seek God about the new, unique thing He wants you to accomplish with your CDC. Don't just look at what someone else is doing. If I had only copied others, we would not have had the mediation program at WACDC. That program was so successful that not only did it serve our clients in excellence, but it also funded our real estate. Another example is when I flew to Boise, Idaho, and got Albertson's to put a grocery store in our urban community. They had never built one in the city. I told them we had a wonderful community for them. They came and every single employee they hired came from our community. That was the Lord positioning me. He gave me a quirky brain to see things a little differently from other people. I'm not saying I'm brave; I am often afraid, but my mother used to tell me, "You don't need courage if you're not afraid, so why don't you do it?" So sometimes, I have to pick up my courage and just do it.

Working together with the community and the amazing assets it contained, by God's grace, we transformed the Crenshaw community from a place people wanted to escape into a destination place that people are now talking about gentrifying.

This work and this Christian CDC represent an effort by believers in Jesus Christ to reach out in witness and ministry based on the conviction that the Gospel of Jesus Christ is relevant to and able to significantly impact the community in which they live and serve.

—DR. LULA BAILEY BALLTON

ABOUT

DR. LULA BAILEY BALLTON

LULA BAILEY BALLTON is Director of Community and Economic Development for the Church of God in Christ International. Dr. Ballton also assists faith-based institutions, churches, CDCs, and nonprofits to identify and leverage their assets to create wealth for their communities through her independent consultancy firm, Lula Ballton and Associates. She is CEO Emeritus where she was a founder and the former President and Chief Executive Officer of the West Angeles Community Development Corporation (CDC), a nonprofit, community-based Development Corporation that operates within the greater ministry of West Angeles Church of God In Christ, under the pastorate of Bishop Charles E. Blake Sr.

As Founder and Executive Director, Dr. Ballton led the West Angeles CDC to receive numerous awards for cutting-edge programs, including: a Best Practices Award from the U.S. Department of Housing and Urban Development for its signature affordable housing project, West A Homes; a Presidential Commendation for its dispute resolution programs; and state, county, and city-wide recognition for its social service, housing, and economic development programs. She served as a Commissioner for the Los Angeles Community Redevelopment Agency (CRA), appointed by Mayor Antonio Villaraigosa and confirmed by the Los Angeles City Council.

Lula Ballton's commitment to education and advocacy for the

poor and the oppressed began at the feet of her Christian family as a child. She participated in the famed March on Washington with Dr. Martin Luther King Jr., as a teenager. After graduating with honors from Central High School in Springfield, Missouri, she attended California State University at Los Angeles, where she earned a B.A. in Speech Communication. After completing undergraduate studies, she was admitted to the prestigious Graduate School of Speech at Northwestern University, where she received an M.A. in Communications.

Dr. Ballton embarked on a successful career as an educator, and, over the next 14 years, held positions as a professor or administrator at Delaware State University, the City Colleges of Chicago, Los Angeles City College, El Camino College, and Loyola Marymount University. She also served as Director of Education for the Chicago Urban League, where she developed policy, programs, and constituency. Dr. Ballton founded the League's Whitney M. Young Scholarship and the Edwin Berry Loan Fund. In 1987 she returned to academia as a student and earned a Juris Doctorate in 1990 from UCLA School of Law. She practiced law at the California State Department of Justice, Civil Rights Division; and Bryan, Cave, McPheeters and McRoberts, a large corporate firm. From there, she entered full-time ministry at the Union Rescue Mission.

A 1999 graduate of Harvard Divinity School Summer Leadership Institute (SLI), she has been both a Harvard Divinity School SLI lecturer and advisory board member. Currently, Dr. Ballton is a public arbitrator on the neutral roster of NASD Dispute Resolution. She is also a teacher-mentor at the University of Southern California (USC) in the School of Religion and Civic Culture "Cecil Murray Passing the Mantle" program.

Dr. Ballton continues to be active in civil rights, and is or was a member of the following boards and civic and professional organizations: Harvard Divinity School, Leadership Council; Wells

Fargo Community Advisory Council; Southern California Edison Advisory Board; National Congress of Community Economic Developers; Northwestern University's prestigious "Committee of 100"; Vanguard University Board of Trustees; Christian Community Development Association, Board of Directors; Churches United for Economic Development, Board of Directors; Black Women Lawyers; The Links, Inc., IPC Chapter; and The Links White Rose Foundation, Board of Directors; the U.S. Department of Justice–Drug Enforcement Administration, Advisory Committee; Leadership California honoree; Commissioner of the Los Angeles Community Redevelopment Agency; and a Fellow at the National Organization of Black Legislative Elected Women. She is a member of and served on the Advisory Board of the Alpha Kappa Alpha Educational Advancement Foundation, Inc.; Leaders Up Board Member; and Chaplain of the International Black Women's Public Policy Institute.

Dr. Ballton is a sought-after speaker and an accomplished writer. Her articles appear in numerous publications, including the *National Black Law Journal*. Her books include: *50 Saturdays Before You Say I Do: Plan Your Marriage, Not Just Your Wedding*; *Sittin' Around Bein' Brown*, a collection of short stories; and *Sister to Sister, Volume II: Devotions for African-American Women* (Judson Press).

She has received numerous honors and awards, including: *LA Business Journal's* nomination for "Women Who Make a Difference;" "Women of Excellence Award" by The National Center for Strategic Nonprofit Planning and Community Leadership; the Jenesse Center's Silver Rose Award; National Association of Black History's "Women of Distinction Award;" Los Angeles Urban League's "Distinguished Community Service Award"; honored by The California Reinvestment Coalition; selected as a KJLH Radio "Proven Achiever"; honoree of The Greater Los Angeles African-American Chamber of Commerce's (GLAAACC) 13th Annual Economic Awards

Dinner; the "Deborah Award" by the Anti-Defamation League; chosen as a panelist on University of Southern California's panel, sponsored by the John Templeton Foundation, "Pentecostalism's Spiritual Capital in Los Angeles"; honored by Women In Ministry of the Southern California Conference of the African Methodist Episcopal Church at a "Living Legends Luncheon" for her life-changing work in the community. Dr. Ballton was also awarded the Community Visionary Award by the Social Enterprise Alliance, and she has been selected as a Los Angeles City College Alumnus of the year.

Dr. Ballton has been married to Carl Ballton, retired President and Chief Executive Officer of the MUFG Union Bank Foundation and Managing Director of MUFG Union Bank, since 1969. She is the mother of three: Jabari, Issa Carl, and Micah, and the grandmother of Caleb, Cameron, Cason, Noah, Lailah, Jaxon, and Jabari Carl.

RAE LYNNE JOHNSON

A recognized and respected writing expert, Rae Lynne has taught and coached writing for over 25 years. She has a gift not only to simplify this complex subject but to quickly activate the writing potential in her students and clients. Those who experience the opportunity to work with her are transformed, not just in their writing, but in their confidence, creativity, and power.

After graduating from the University of Southern California, Rae Lynne was trained and employed at the Institute of Reading Development to teach high-energy reading and writing classes designed to instill lifelong competency and enthusiasm.

A master teacher, Rae Lynne went on to create her own writing classes, workshops, seminars, and retreats, developing an engaging and effective curriculum infused with her love of writing. Her fiction and nonfiction programs help her clients produce vivid, compelling writing they can be proud of, writing that represents them well in the marketplace of ideas.

Whether presenting to executives or leading a weekend retreat, Rae Lynne stops at nothing to exhilarate and unlock her clients. She has helped hundreds release their unique voices and share their stories and messages with passion, purpose, and power. Her most recent contribution as a writer is the group of staff profiles and other segments of *Extraordinary Ministry in Ordinary Places: A Guide to Christian Community Development*.

Rae Lynne lives in Los Angeles where she cofounded an editing business with her husband, James. They have four children, all writers. Workshopping stories, scripts, and books is a never-ending, exuberant family affair in her household.

CONTRIBUTORS

Ariel Bailey Fernald

Ariel Fernald is a born peacemaker who lives out her call as a mediator, minister, and producer of live theater and film productions that seek to influence our world to live at peace with God and each other. Ariel helped to create and is the first graduate with a Peace Studies major from Chapman University. She established her own consulting company Conflict Management Services and went on to help found and direct three nonviolence mediation centers in Southern California, including Mediation and Restitution Services, Community Non-violence Resource Center, and eventually, the West Angeles Community Resource Center. These centers provided mediation, training, and program development for individuals and community organizations.

Ariel currently mediates and consults in conflict management while serving as the Cofounder and President of Eastern Sky Theatre Company (ESTC) alongside her husband, Trey. Through ESTC they have shared the Gospel and other life changing truths in their works. Ariel is a multiple award-winning filmmaker. Throughout her life Ariel has been active in her church and the community ministering as the Lord leads her. She is married to her college sweetheart and they have three beautiful children.

Claudia L. Jones

Claudia L. Jones is a native of Los Angeles, California, who relocated to the Atlanta, Georgia, area in 2008. With over 30 years of professional experience, Ms. Jones has dedicated her career to working in the nonprofit arena. Although retired, she is contractually employed as a Domestic Violence Advocate and Monitor for court-or-dered child visitations.

As the Chief Operating Officer for the West Angeles Communi-ty Development Corporation (WACDC) in Los Angeles for almost 15 years, Ms. Jones oversaw the administrative and fiscal opera-tions of the organization and was responsible for coordination of the Department Manager's duties. Ms. Jones is one of the found-ers and former board members of the Compton/Watts Interfaith Collaborative Inc. and has served on the FEMA-EFSP (Emergen-cy Food and Shelter Program) Allocations Board. She earned a BA in Organization Management from Vanguard University in Costa Mesa, California, where she graduated *summa cum laude*. She then completed her MA at Antioch University-Los Angeles in Organiza-tional/Business Management.

Paul H. Turner

Paul has been a champion for social and economic justice for more than two decades. Prior to his appointment as the Development Co-Worker with the Community of Disciples of Christ in Congo (CDCC) through the Common Global Ministries of The Christian Church (Disciples of Christ) and United Church of Christ in DR Congo, he was an established leader in faith-based community development. He has been responsible for building affordable housing, creating social enterprises, and advocating for greater community reinvestment in low-income communities from financial institutions.

In his work in DR Congo, Paul worked directly with CDCC pastors and church leaders in their efforts to sustain and expand pro-grams in the areas of community development, women's empower-ment, economic development, education, and public health. Paul also served three years as President of Save Africa's Children (SAC), a faith-based, nonprofit organization with a mission to expand the scope of care for orphan and vulnerable children impacted by HIV-AIDS in Sub-Saharan Africa. Prior to SAC he directed community reinvestment activities in low-to-moderate income communities in Southern California for Citigroup. At the Greenlining Institute, Paul worked to advance civil rights, equal opportunity and diversity in California and across the country. Paul received his BA in Political Economy from Bethany College, and his MS in Global Economic Development from Eastern University.

Robert J. Norris Jr.

Robert is currently employed as Principal Analyst at the Fort Ord Reuse Authority (FORA) with responsibility for staffing the FORA Veterans Issues Advisory Committee. Before working at West Angeles CDC, he was employed as Executive Vice President of the Century Housing Corporation in Los Angeles. Century Housing produced over 14,000 units of affordable housing in the Los Angeles area. At Century, he was active in the conversion of the former Long Beach Naval Base to the Century Villages at Cabrillo, a multi-phase transitional to permanent housing village in partnership with public and private organizations throughout the region. He is a 2011 recipient of the White House Community Drum Major Award for his work with the Faith-Based Community.

Robert has undergraduate degrees in Political Science and Black Studies from the University of California, Santa Barbara. He has an MA in Organizational Development and has completed the City of San Diego Management Academy for Senior Executives. Robert is a combat veteran with service in the U.S. Marine Corps in Viet Nam. He is a graduate of the Defense Language Institute in Monterey, and currently is completing ten years on the Board of Directors of the National Coalition for Homeless Veterans. He also is The Area

Commander of the National Association of Black Veterans. Married to Theresa (Teri) Norris, he and his wife have four sons who are all college graduates.

Samuel K. Hughes

Sam Hughes is an entrepreneur and manager of economic and real estate development with over 25 years of related experience straddling the public and private sectors. Currently, he leads the Economic Development Division staff as Assistant General Manager of the Economic and Workforce Development Department (EWDD) for the City of Los Angeles. The division is dedicated to helping EWDD fulfill its mission of stimulating LA's economy by leveraging resources to create and retain sustainable jobs and businesses that improve the quality of life for residents and enhance the City's tax base. The division manages a portfolio of real estate developments, business loans, redevelopment improvements, and other community enhancement projects throughout Los Angeles.

Sam has a BA from UCLA and holds certificates from the University of Southern California Program in Real Estate and Cal Poly Pomona Program in Construction Management. He is a board member of several economic development corporations and is often called upon to speak at economic development conferences. He is married with two sons and resides in California.

Sandra M. Speed

Sandra Speed is the Regional Diverse Segments Manager for Wells Fargo Home Mortgage. In this role, she develops strategic and tactical plans to grow loan production in diverse segment markets. She has created successful business partnerships with realtors, builders, housing agencies, and nonprofit organizations to increase home purchase production for first-time homebuyers and low- and moderate-income (LMI) and minority homebuyers in Orange County and San Diego County, California.

Sandra has served as the Project Manager, Developer, and Consultant on numerous housing development projects and has an extensive background in the development of affordable and market rate housing. She previously served as an appointee of the Pasadena City Council to the Northwest Commission and was on the City of Pasadena's Housing Subcommittee.

Sandra is an instructor, speaker, and published author whose articles have appeared in *Business Life Magazine, Pasadena Star News,* and the *Orange County Register*. She is a board member of Affordable Housing Clearinghouse (AHC), Board Treasurer for the Urban League of San Diego County, and is the former Vice President of the Orange County Association of Real Estate Professionals.

Tunua Thrash-Ntuk

A native Angeleno, Tunua Thrash-Ntuk is the Executive Director of the Los Angeles Local Initiatives Support Corporation (LA LISC). She is a seasoned community and economic development practitioner of more than 15 years with both nonprofit and private sector experiences. Her strengths range from community advocacy to asset and real estate development around neighborhood revitalization. She has already led a number of important urban initiatives in Los Angeles focused on affordable housing and commercial development as well as transit-oriented projects. Prior to joining LISC, Tunua served as Executive Director of the West Angeles Community Development Corporation. During her tenure, she was responsible for the asset management and oversight of the WACDC real estate portfolio valued at $150 million. Tunua led the growth of WACDC's real estate portfolio, including the development, construction, and opening of West Angeles Plaza, a 24,000-square-foot commercial office project.

Tunua is a graduate of Massachusetts Institute of Technology (MIT) where she earned her Master's in City Planning (MCP) and UC Berkeley where she received her BA in Interdisciplinary Studies.

Made in the
USA
Middletown, DE

77343491R00106